BIG-NOTE PIANO

2ND EDITION

THE BEST OF ANDREW LLOYD WEBBER™

T0052795

ISBN 978-0-6340-0029-4

HAL•LEONARD®
CORPORATION
7777 W. BLUEMOUND RD. P.O. BOX 13819 MILWAUKEE, WI 53213

Visit Hal Leonard Online at
www.halleonard.com

ALL I ASK OF YOU
from THE PHANTOM OF THE OPERA

Music by ANDREW LLOYD WEBBER
Lyrics by CHARLES HART
Additional Lyrics by RICHARD STILGOE

Slowly (in 2)

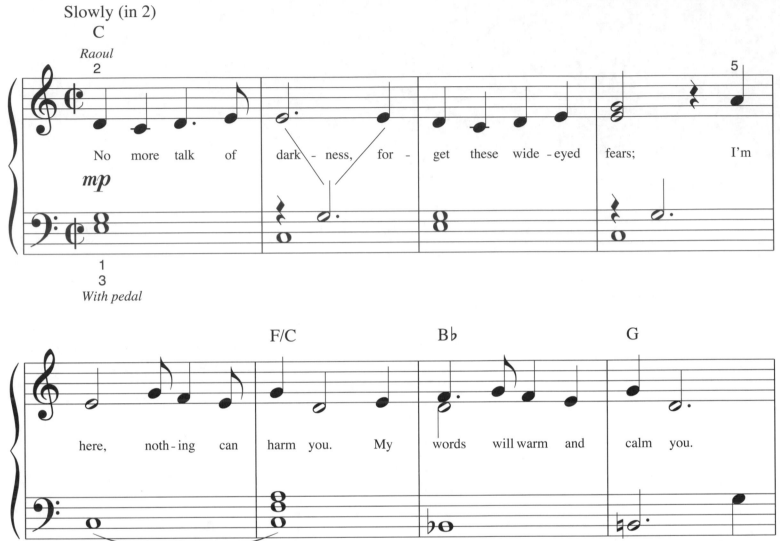

No more talk of dark - ness, for - get these wide - eyed fears; I'm

here, noth - ing can harm you. My words will warm and calm you.

Let me be your free - dom, let day - light dry your tears; I'm

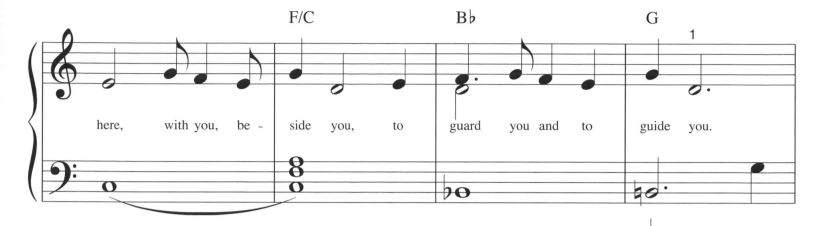

here,   with you, be - side you,   to   guard   you and to   guide you.

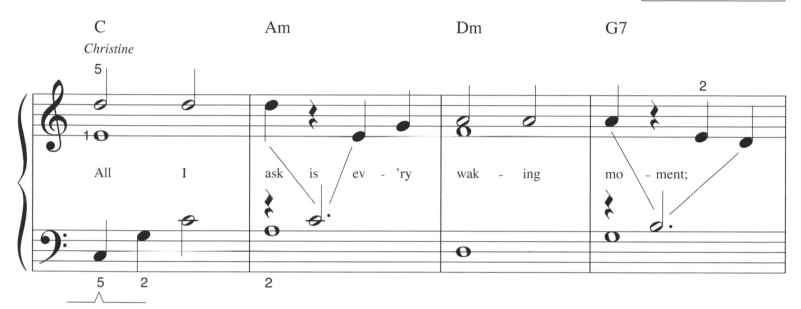

Christine

All   I   ask   is   ev - 'ry   wak   -   ing   mo   - ment;

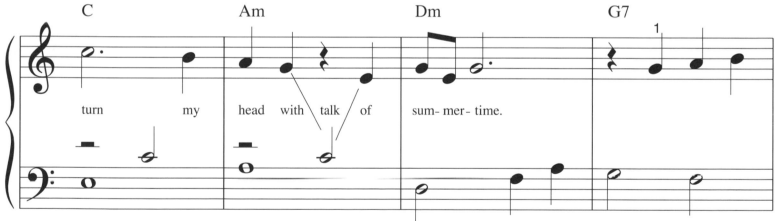

turn   my   head with talk of   sum- mer- time.

Say   you   need me   with you   now   and   al - ways;

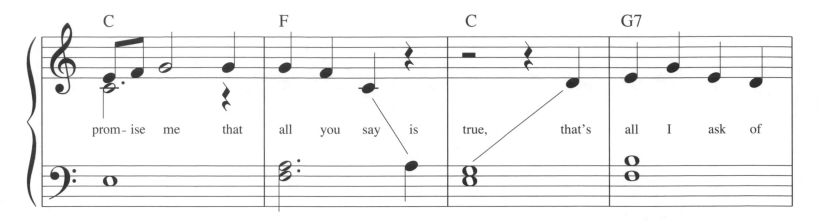

C   F   C   G7

prom- ise me that all you say is true, that's all I ask of

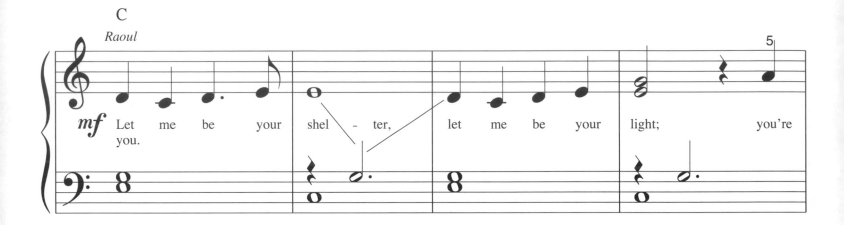

C

Raoul

mf Let me be your shel - ter, let me be your light; you're
you.

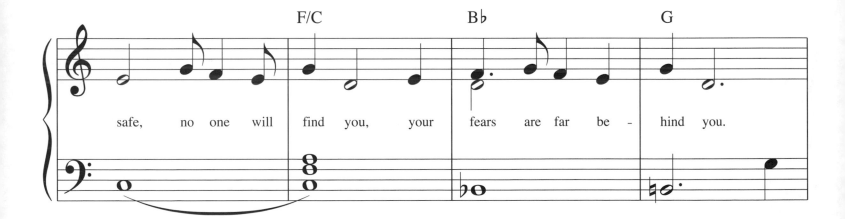

F/C   Bb   G

safe, no one will find you, your fears are far be - hind you.

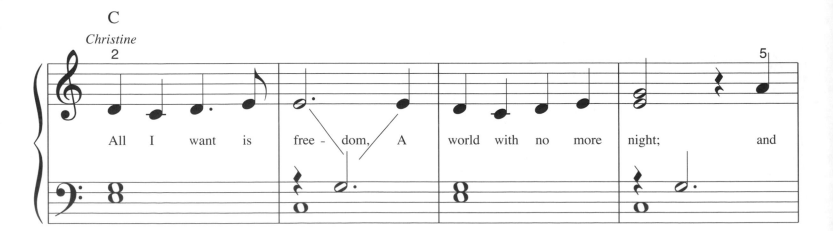

C

Christine

All I want is free - dom, A world with no more night; and

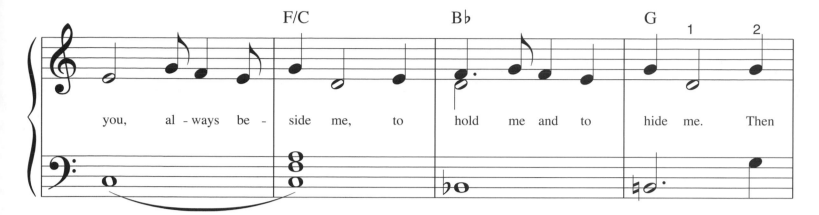

you, al - ways be - side me, to hold me and to hide me. Then

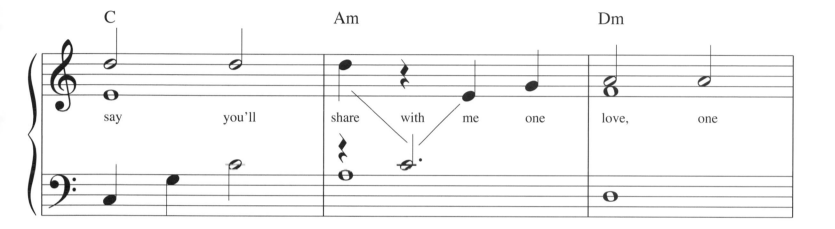

say you'll share with me one love, one

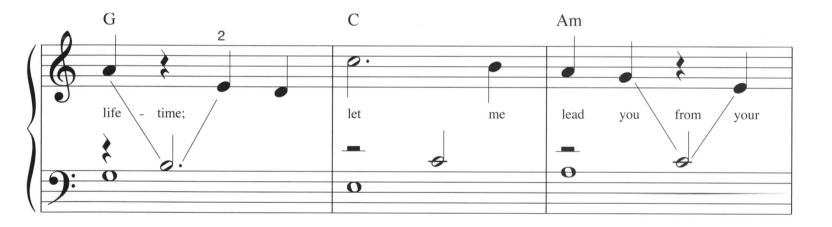

life - time; let me lead you from your

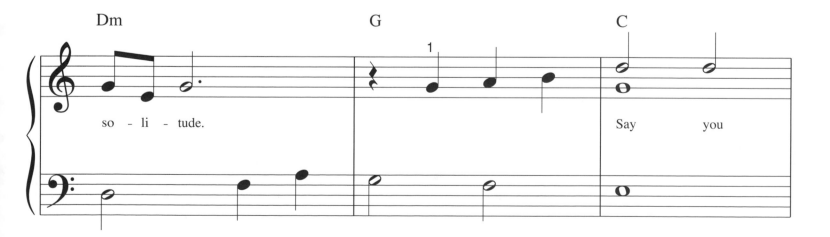

so - li - tude. Say you

6

Am   Dm   G

need me with you, here be - side you,

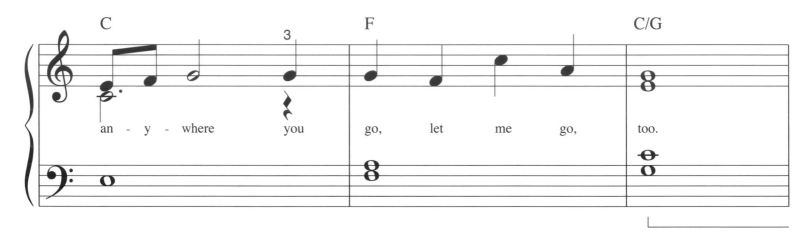

C   F   C/G

an - y - where you go, let me go, too.

Dm   G7   *Christine*   C

Chris - tine, that's all I ask of you. All I

f

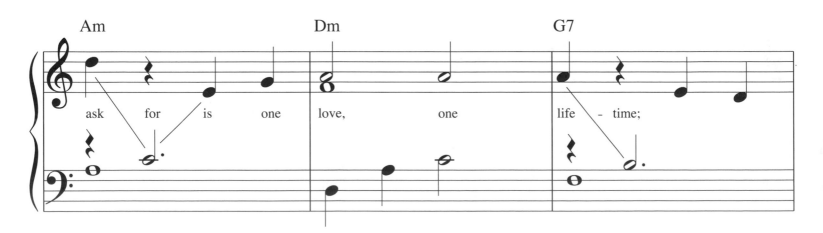

Am   Dm   G7

ask for is one love, one life - time;

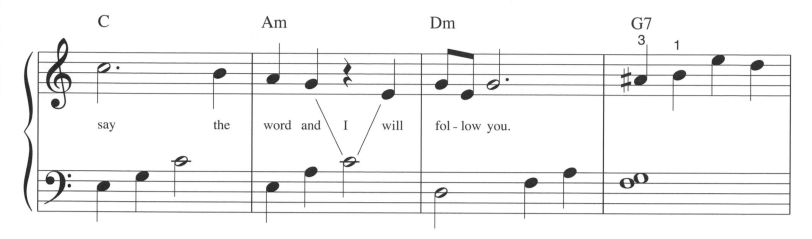

say the word and I will fol - low you.

Share each day with me, each night, each morn - ing.

Slower

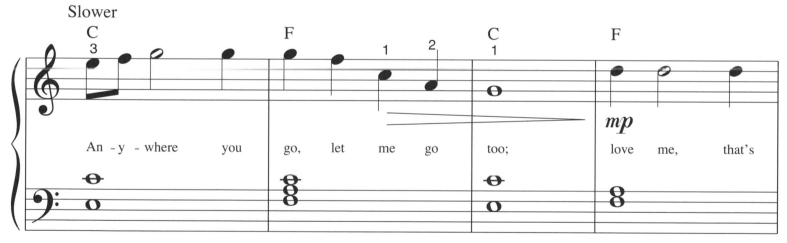

An - y - where you go, let me go too; love me, that's

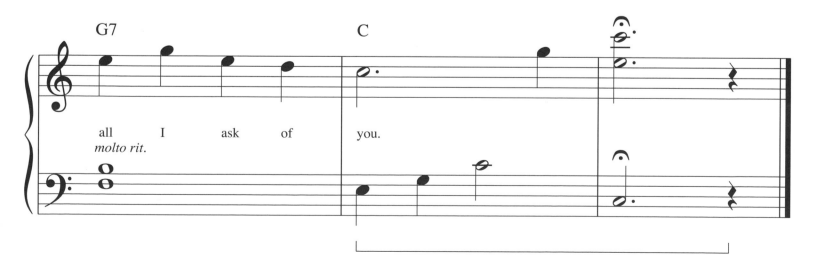

all I ask of you.
molto rit.

ANY DREAM WILL DO

from JOSEPH AND THE AMAZING TECHNICOLOR® DREAMCOAT

Music by ANDREW LLOYD WEBBER
Lyrics by TIM RICE

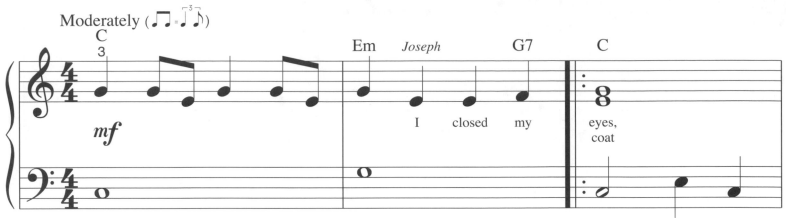

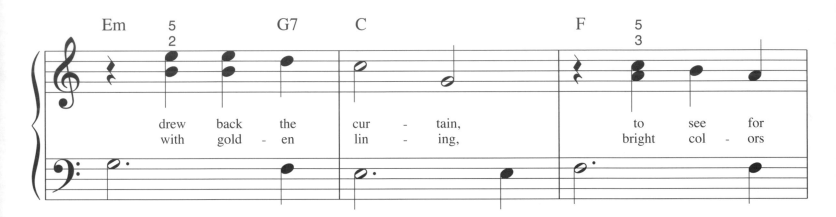

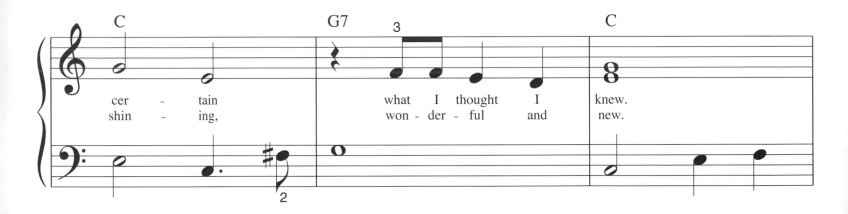

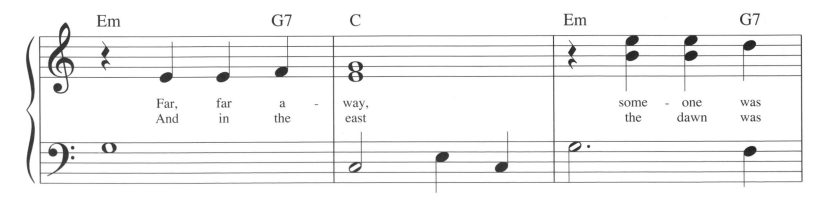

weep - ing,
break - ing,

but the world was sleep - ing.
and the world was wak - ing.

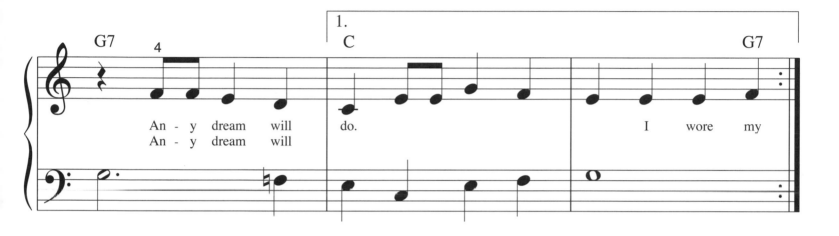

1.

An - y dream will do.
An - y dream will

I wore my

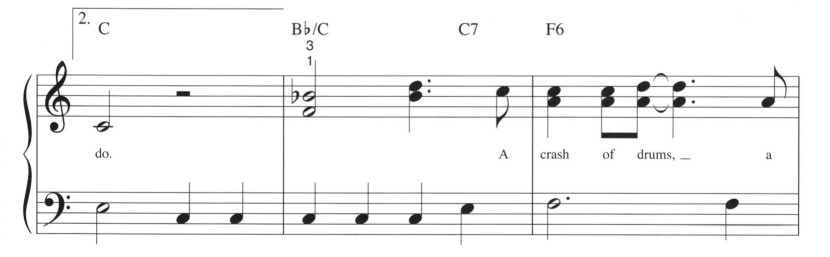

2.

do.

A crash of drums, — a

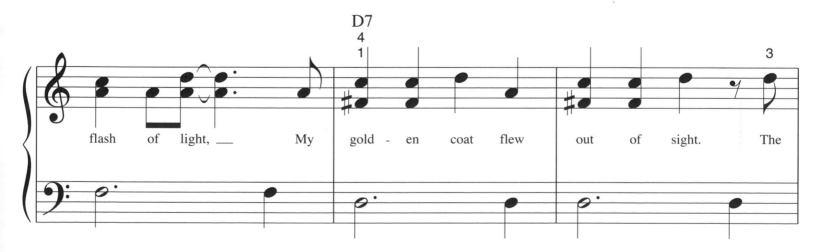

flash of light, — My gold - en coat flew out of sight. The

col - ors fa - ded in - to dark - ness, I was left a -

lone. May I re -

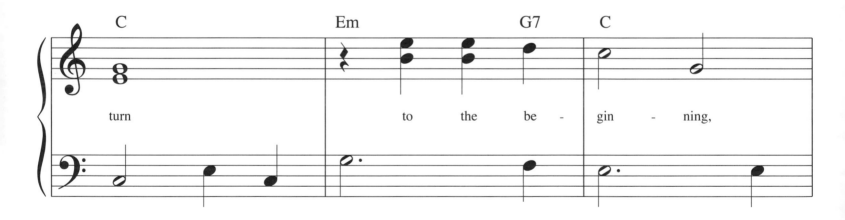

turn to the be - gin - ning,

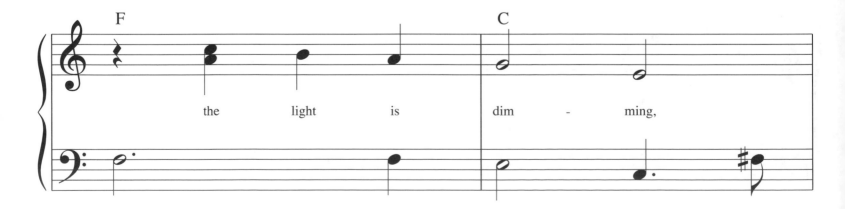

the light is dim - ming,

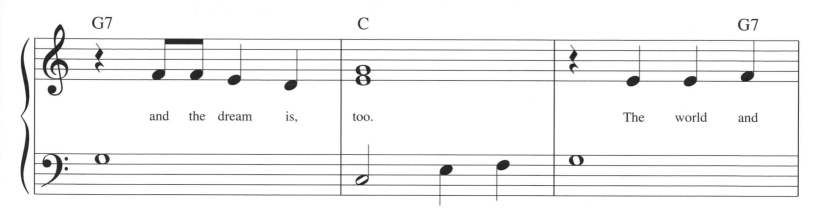

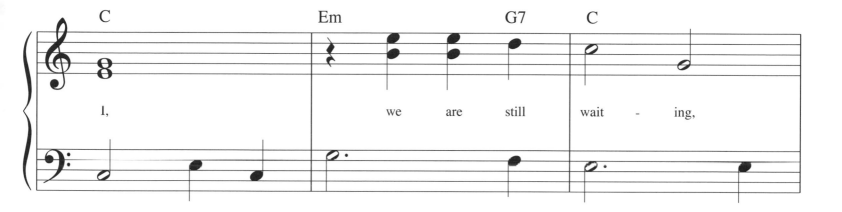

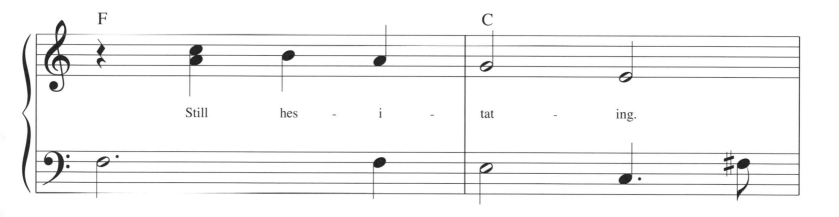

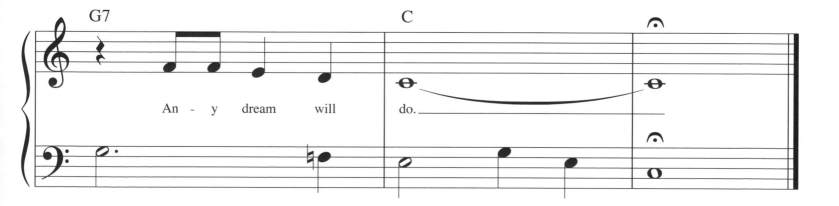

CLOSE EVERY DOOR
from JOSEPH AND THE AMAZING TECHNICOLOR® DREAMCOAT

Music by ANDREW LLOYD WEBBER
Lyrics by TIM RICE

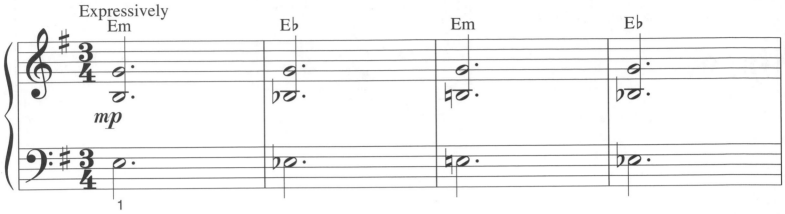

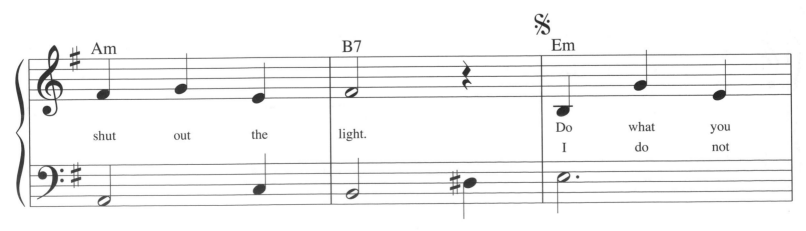

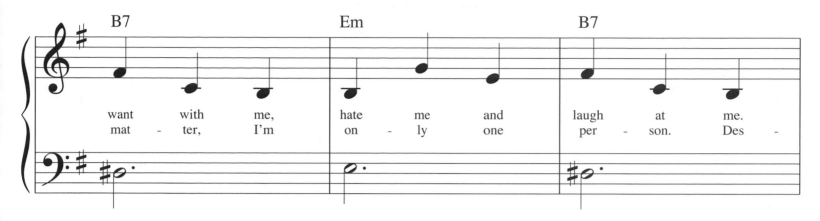

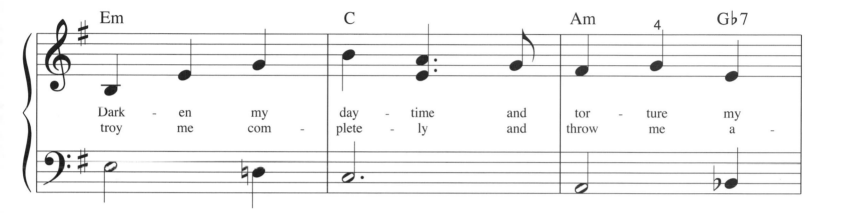

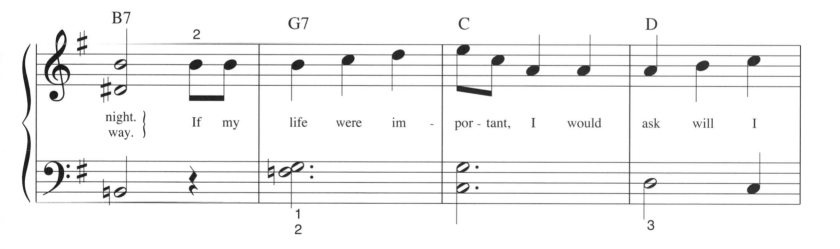

To Coda $\oplus$

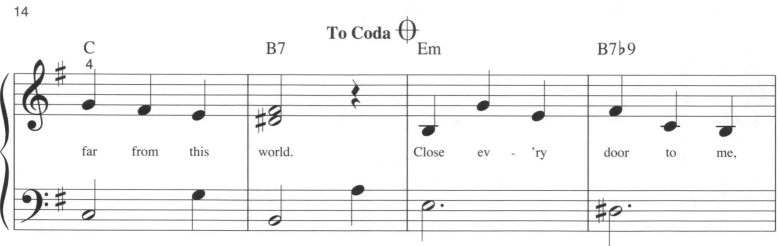

far from this world. Close ev - 'ry door to me,

keep those I love from me. Child - ren of

Is - rael are nev - er a - lone. For I

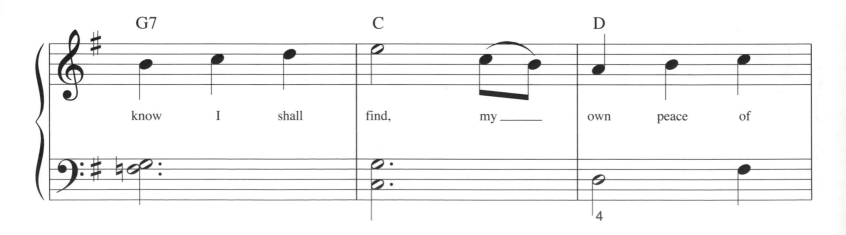

know I shall find, my _____ own peace of

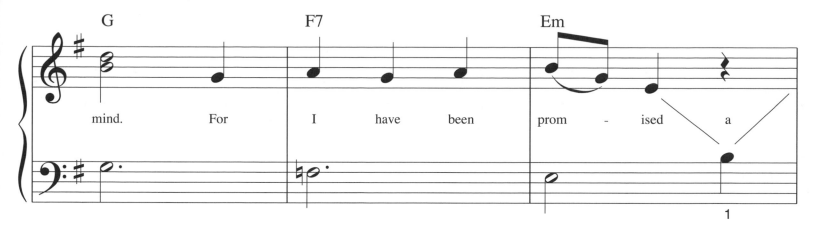

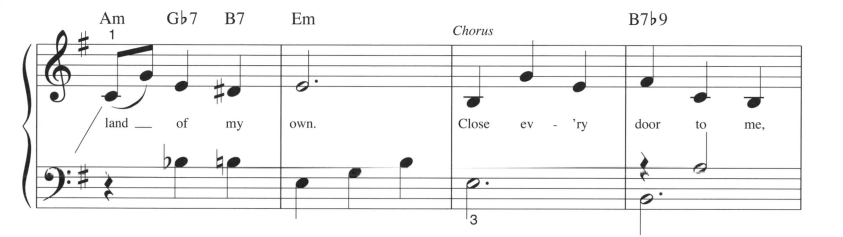

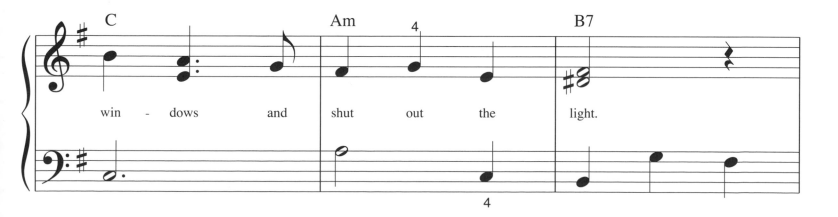

La la la la la la   la la la la la la   la la la la la la

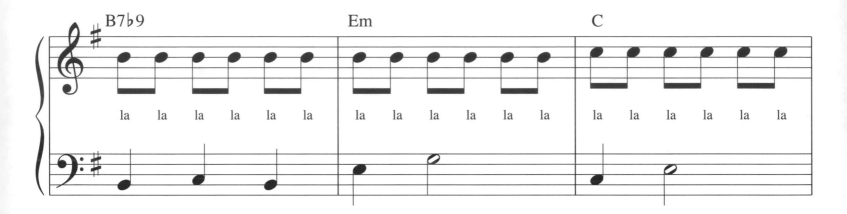

la la la la la la   la la la la la la   la la la la la la

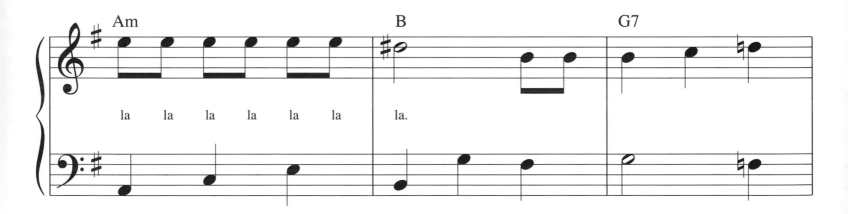

la la la la la la   la.

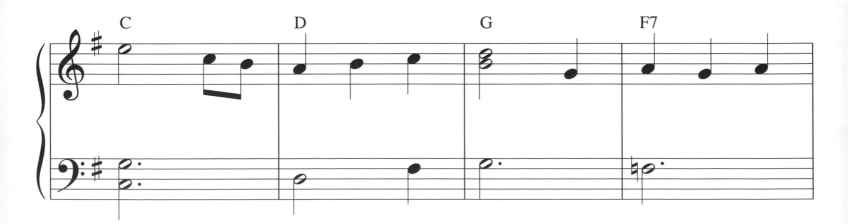

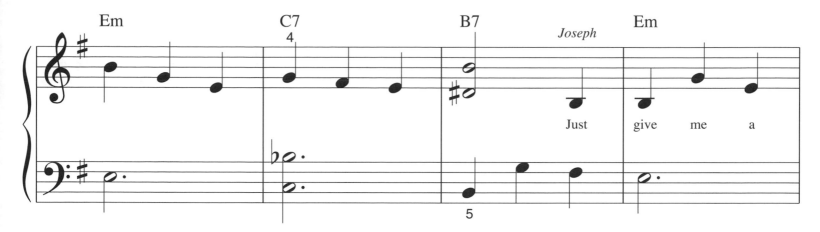

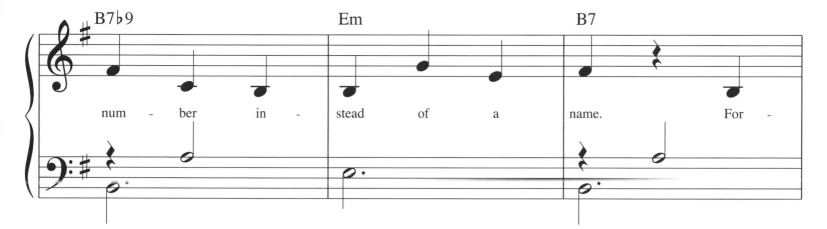

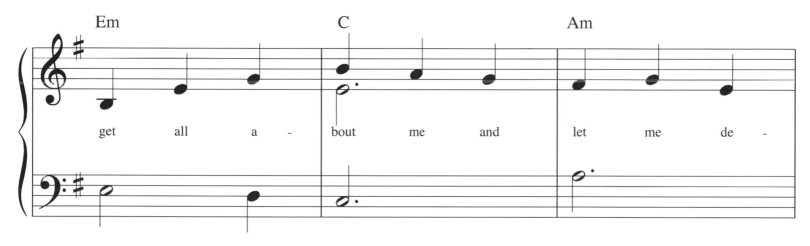

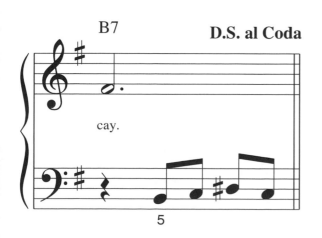

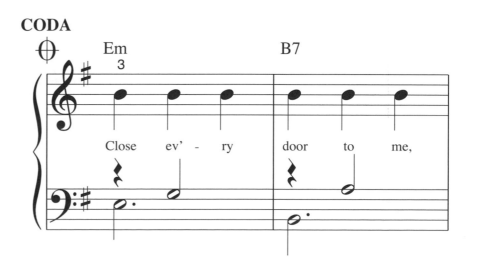

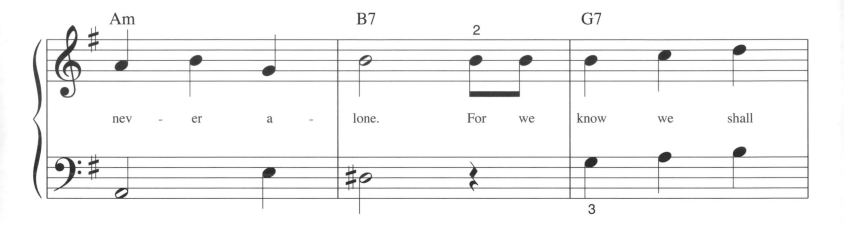

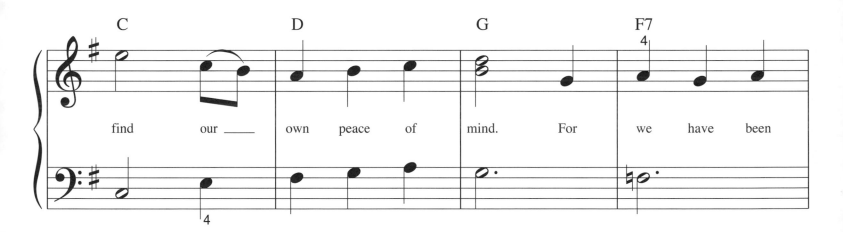

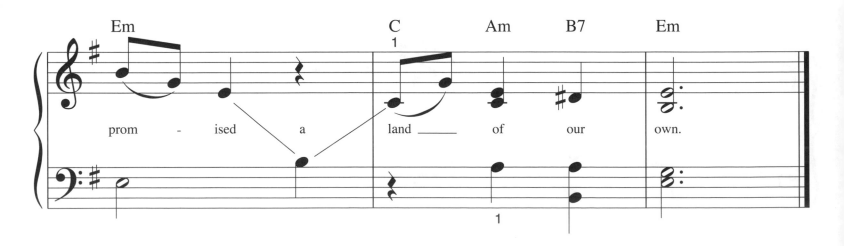

NO MATTER WHAT

from WHISTLE DOWN THE WIND

Music by ANDREW LLOYD WEBBER
Lyrics by JIM STEINMAN

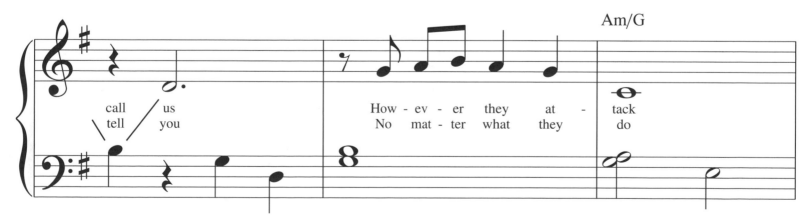

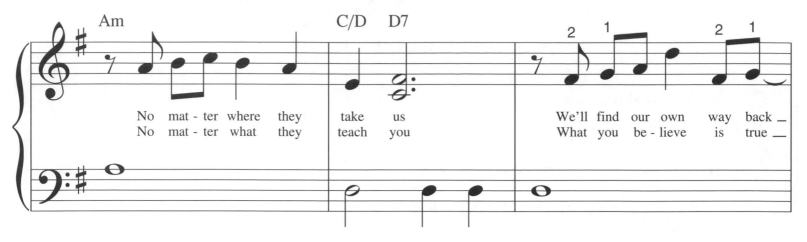

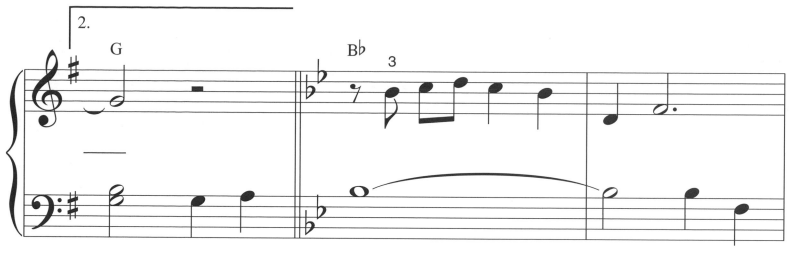

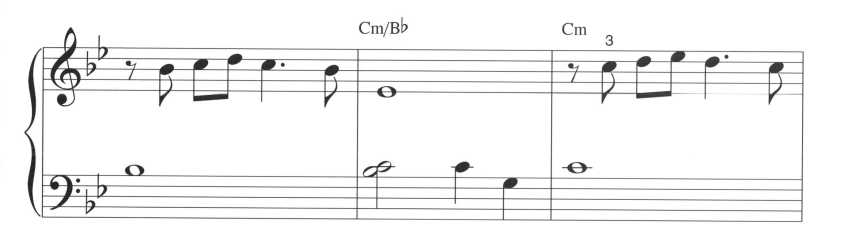

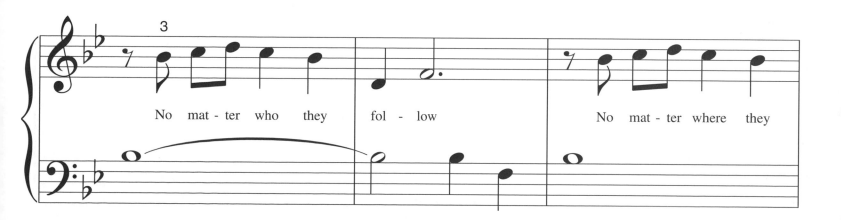

No mat- ter who they fol- low

No mat- ter where they

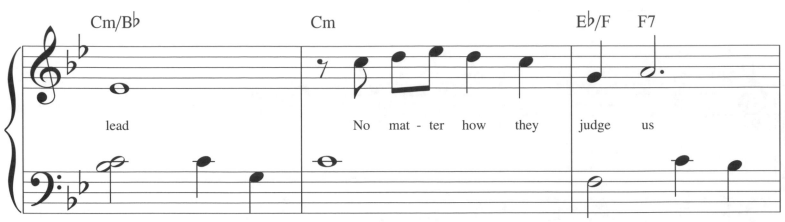

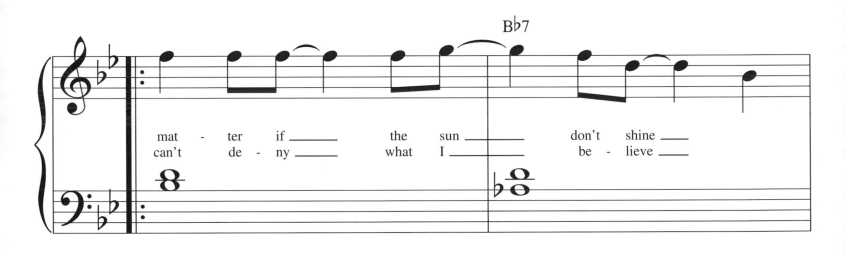

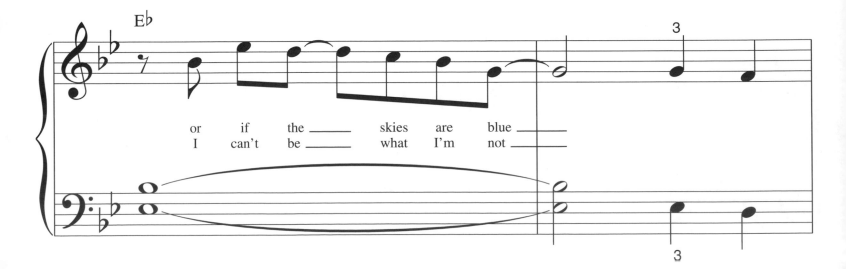

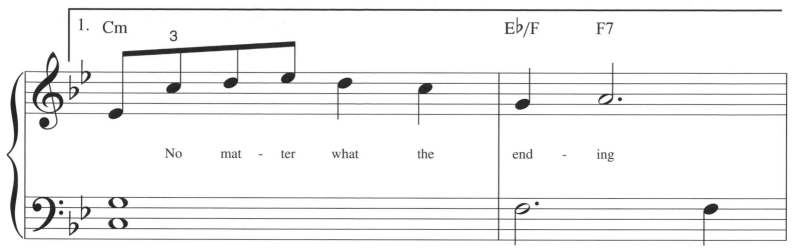

No mat - ter what the end - ing

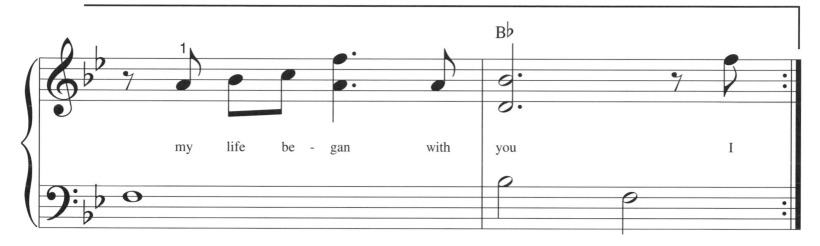

my life be - gan with you I

I know this love's for - ev - er that's all that

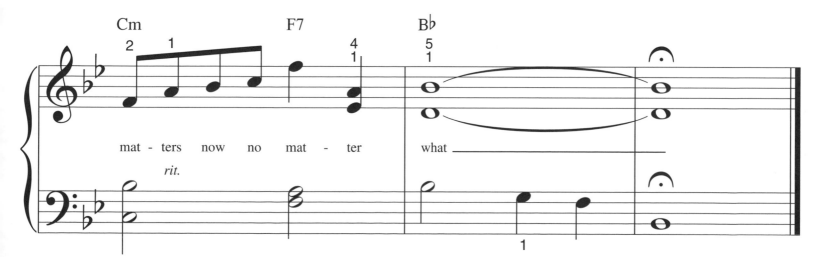

mat - ters now no mat - ter what

DON'T CRY FOR ME ARGENTINA

from EVITA

Words by TIM RICE
Music by ANDREW LLOYD WEBBER

It won't be eas-y, you'll think it strange when I

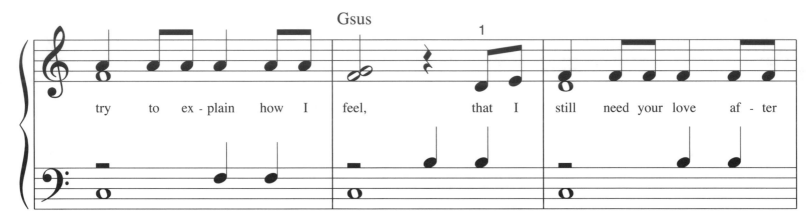

try to ex-plain how I feel, that I still need your love af-ter

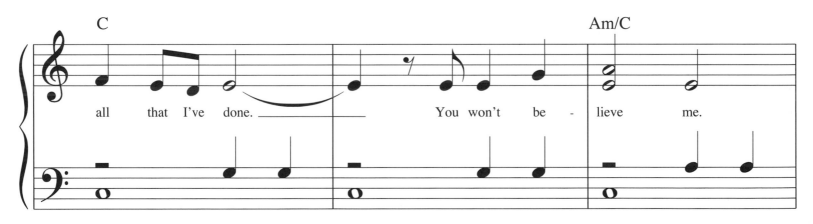

all that I've done. _____ You won't be-lieve me.

All you will see is a girl you once knew, al-though she's dressed up to the

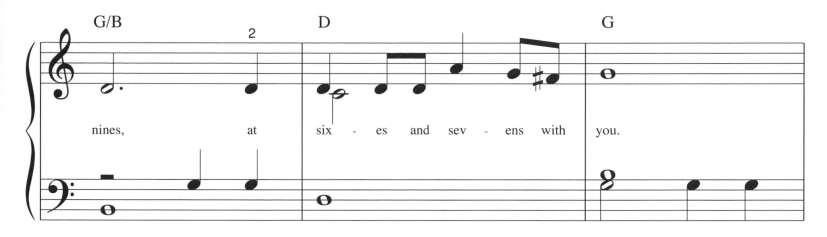

nines, at six - es and sev - ens with you.

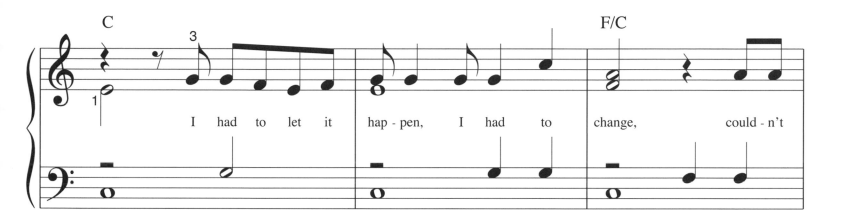

I had to let it hap - pen, I had to change, could - n't

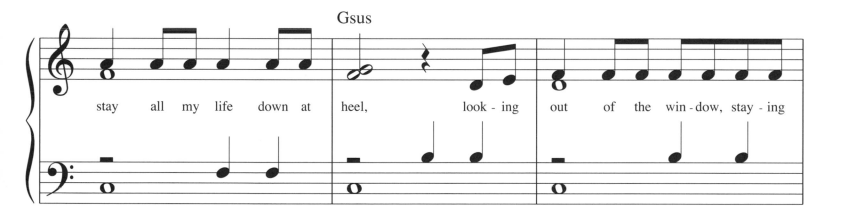

stay all my life down at heel, look - ing out of the win - dow, stay - ing

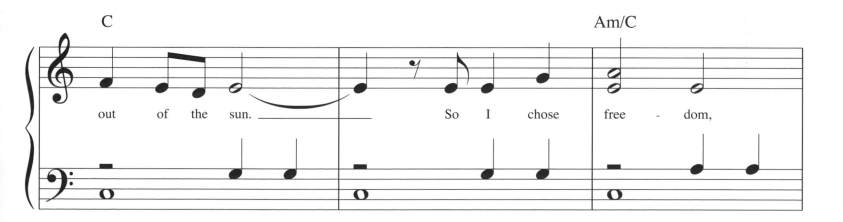

out of the sun. So I chose free - dom,

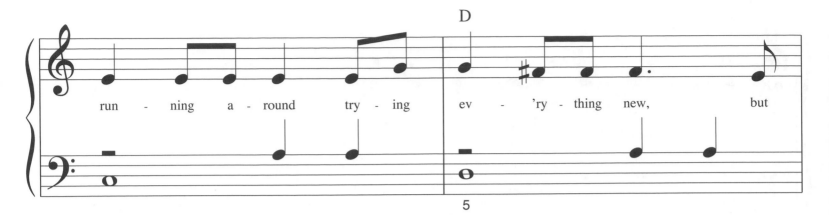

run - ning a - round try - ing ev - 'ry - thing new, but

noth - ing im - pressed me at all. I nev - er ex - pect - ed it

to. Don't cry for me, Ar - gen - ti - na,_____ The

truth is I nev - er left you. All through my wild days, my mad ex -

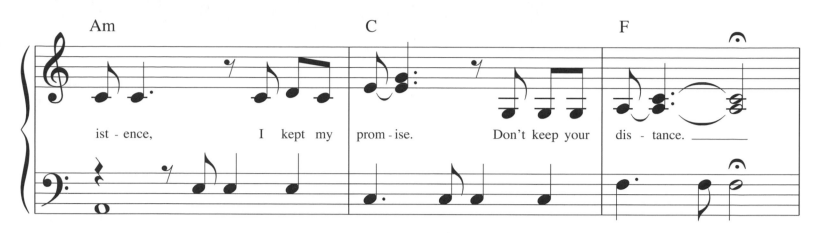

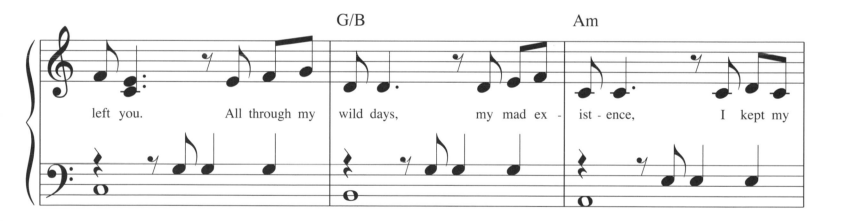

I DON'T KNOW HOW TO LOVE HIM

from JESUS CHRIST SUPERSTAR

Words by TIM RICE
Music by ANDREW LLOYD WEBBER

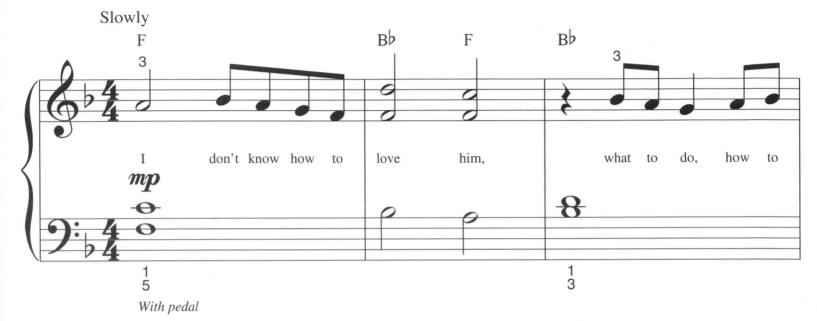

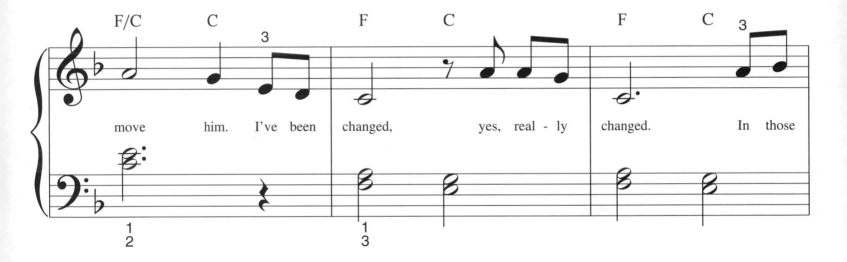

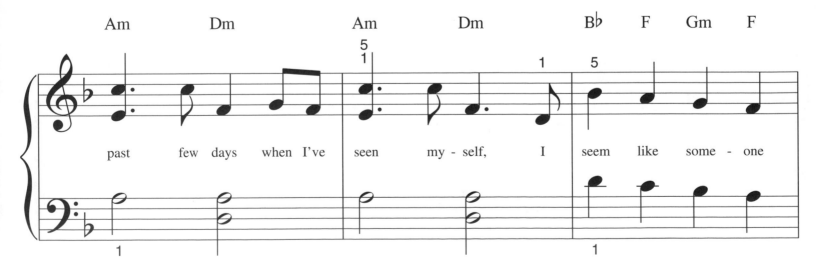

else. I don't know how to take this.

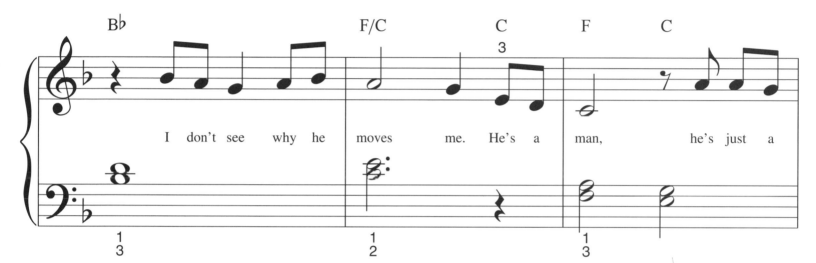

I don't see why he moves me. He's a man, he's just a

man, and I've had so man - y men be - fore, in

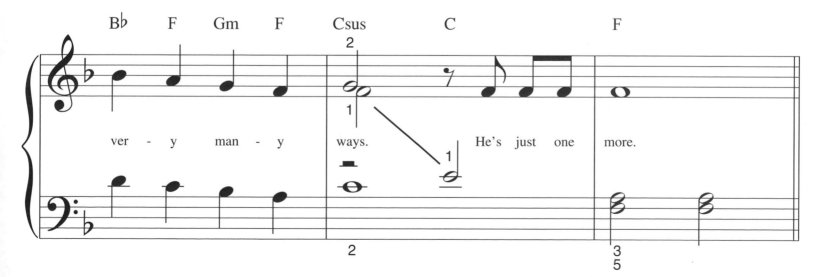

ver - y man - y ways. He's just one more.

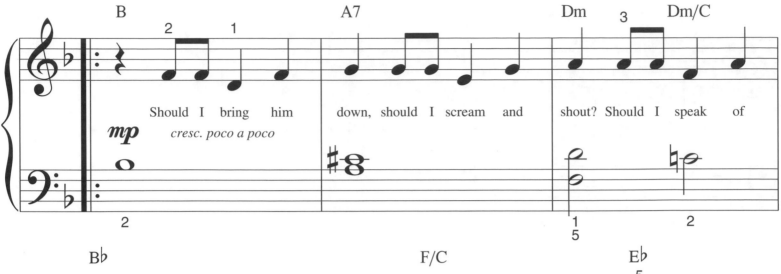

Should I bring him down, should I scream and shout? Should I speak of

mp
cresc. poco a poco

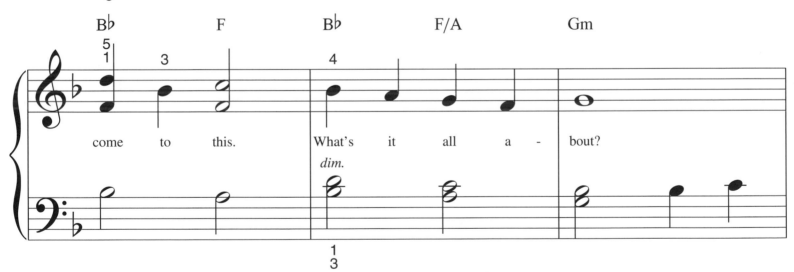

love, let my feel - ings out? I nev - er thought I'd

f

come to this. What's it all a - bout?

dim.

Don't you think it's rath - er fun - ny,
Yet, if he said he loved me,

mp

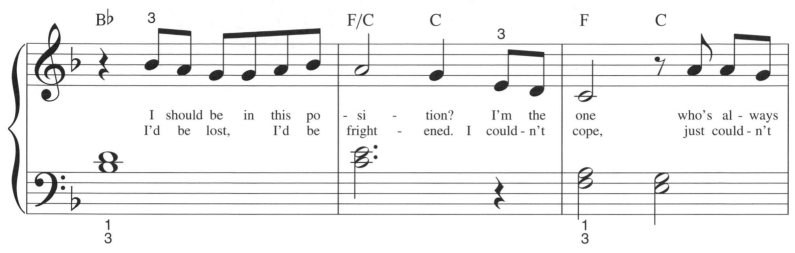

I should be in this po - si - tion? I'm the one who's al - ways
I'd be lost, I'd be fright - ened. I could - n't cope, just could - n't

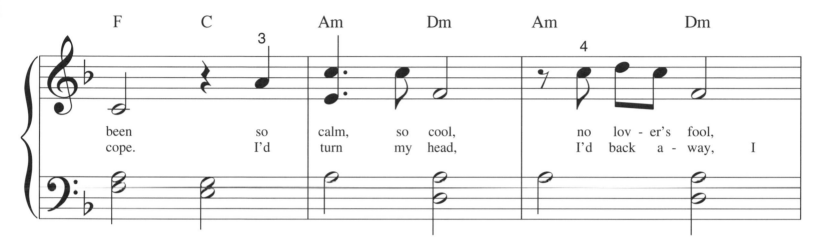

been so calm, so cool, no lov - er's fool,
cope. I'd turn my head, I'd back a - way, I

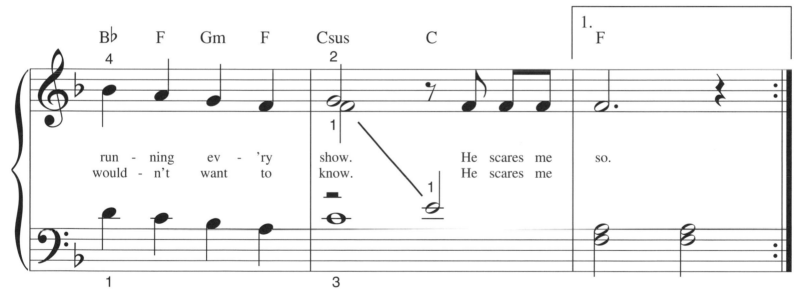

run - ning ev - 'ry show. He scares me so.
would - n't want to know. He scares me

so. I want him so. I love him so.

LEARN TO BE LONELY
from THE PHANTOM OF THE OPERA

Music by ANDREW LLOYD WEBBER
Lyrics by CHARLES HART

Moderately

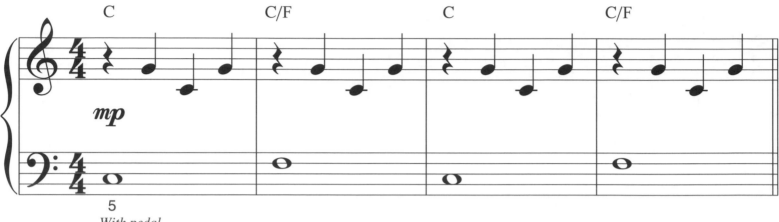

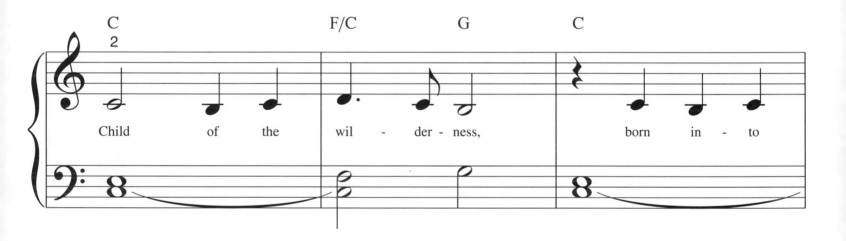

Child of the wil - der - ness, born in - to

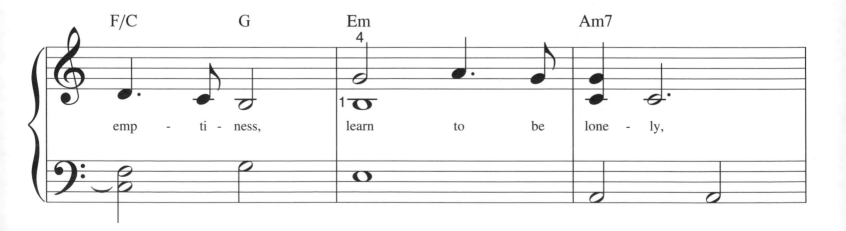

emp - ti - ness, learn to be lone - ly,

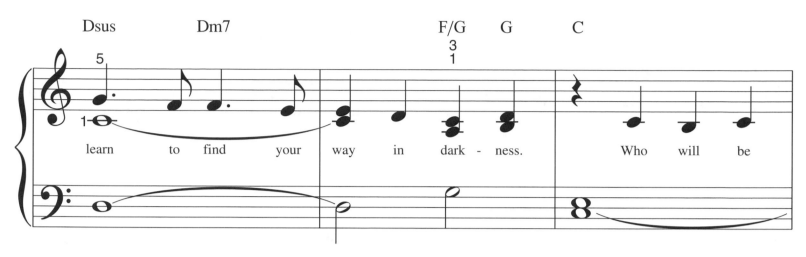

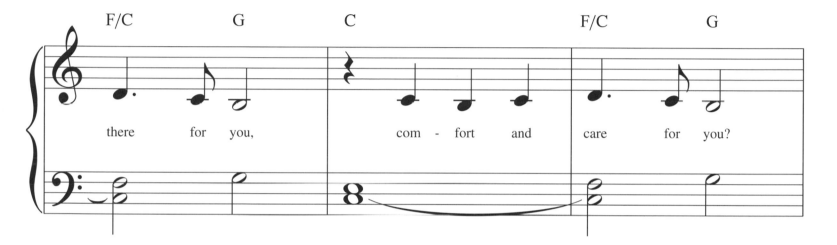

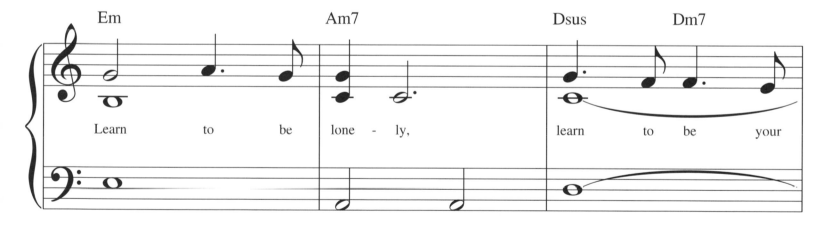

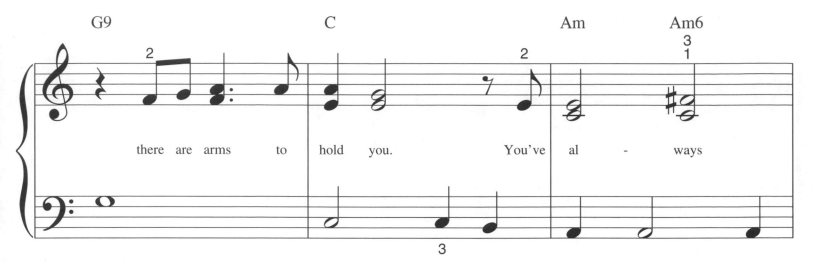

there are arms to hold you. You've al - ways

known your heart was on its own. So

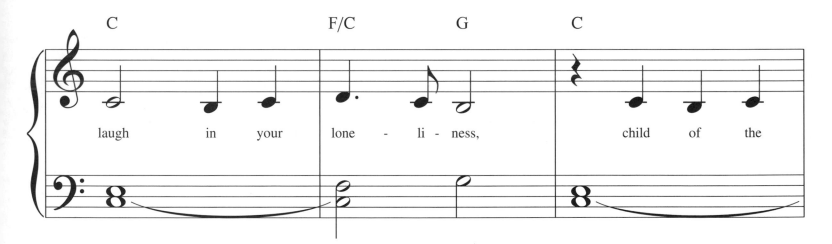

laugh in your lone - li - ness, child of the

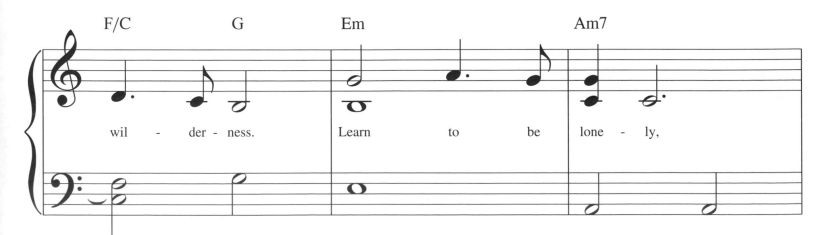

wil - der - ness. Learn to be lone - ly,

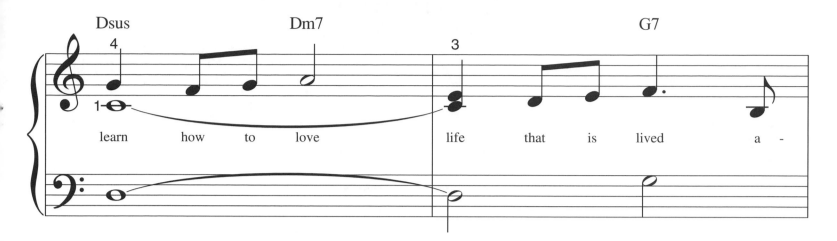

learn how to love life that is lived a -

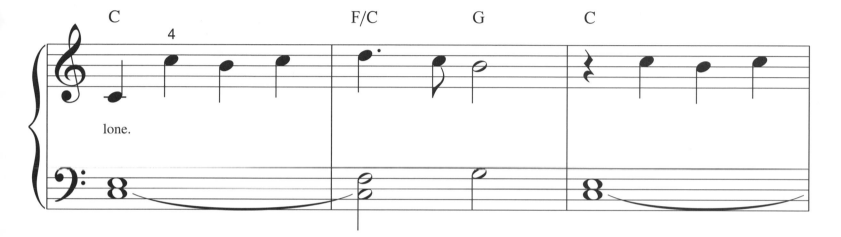

lone.

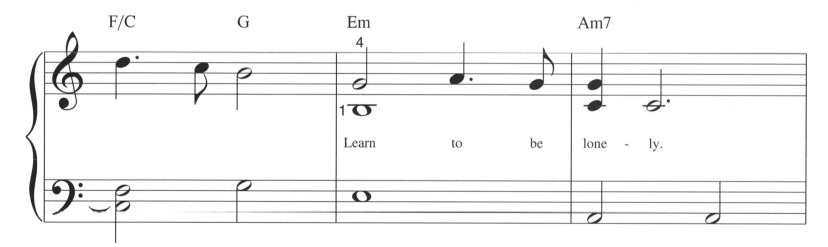

Learn to be lone - ly.

Life can be lived, life can be loved a - lone.

rit.

MEMORY
from CATS

Music by ANDREW LLOYD WEBBER
Text by TREVOR NUNN after T.S. ELIOT

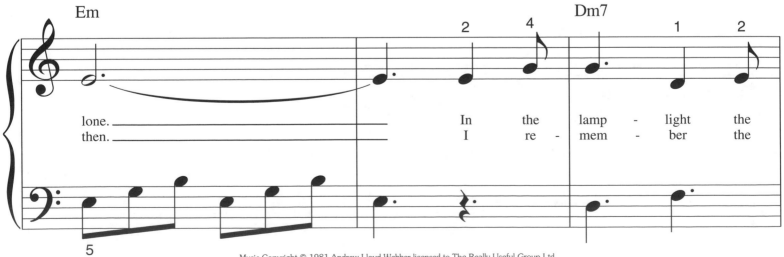

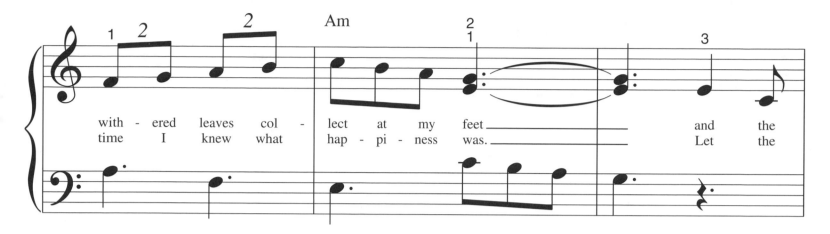

with - ered leaves col - lect at my feet____ and the
time I knew what hap - pi - ness was.____ Let the

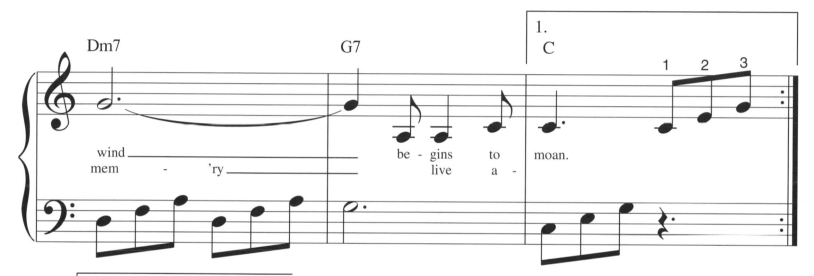

wind____ be - gins to moan.
mem - 'ry____ live a -

gain.

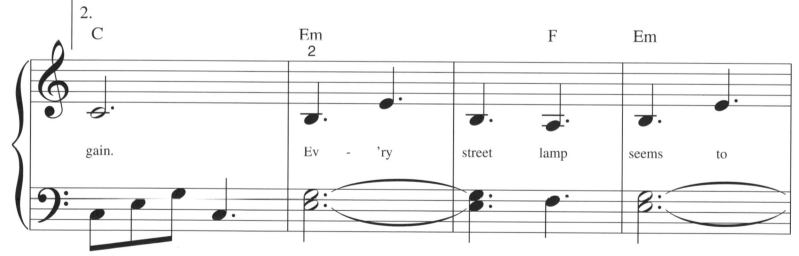

Ev - 'ry street lamp seems to

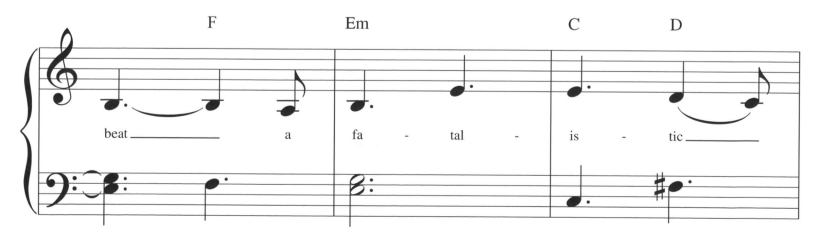

beat____ a fa - tal - is - tic____

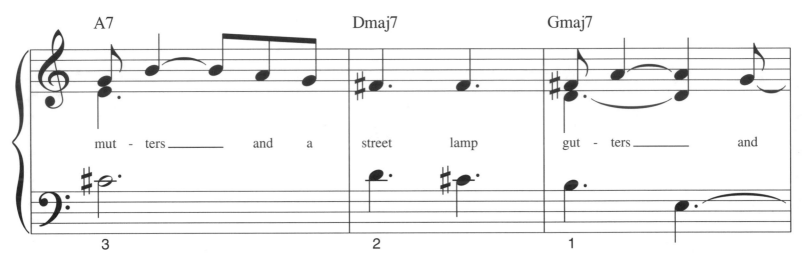

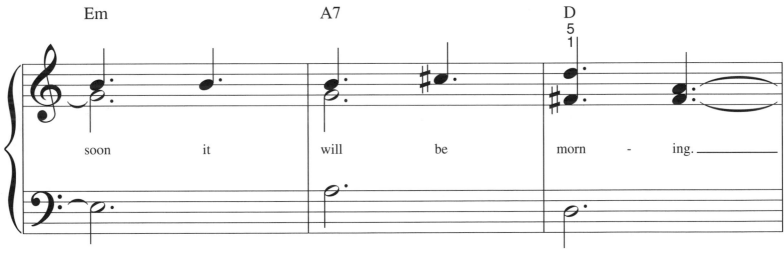

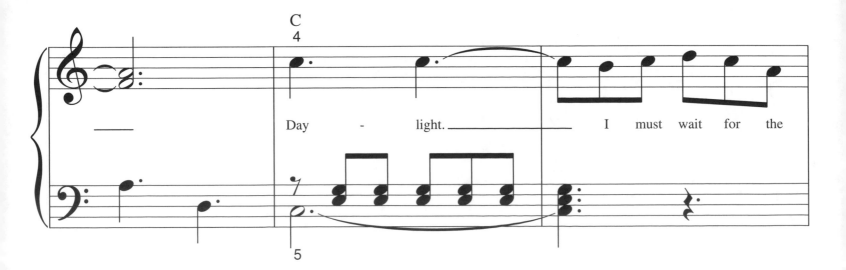

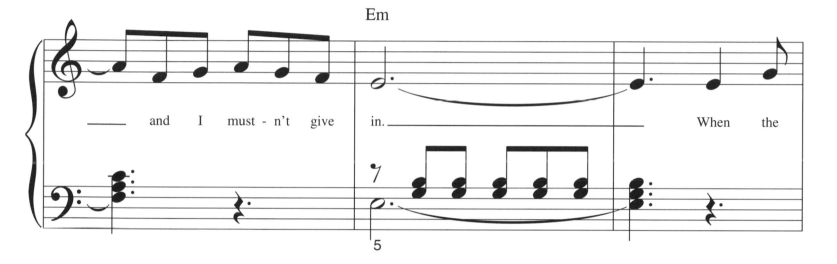

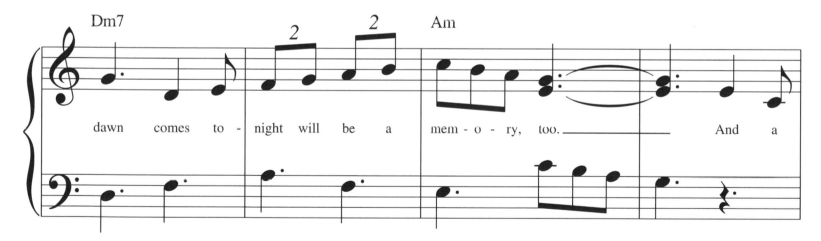

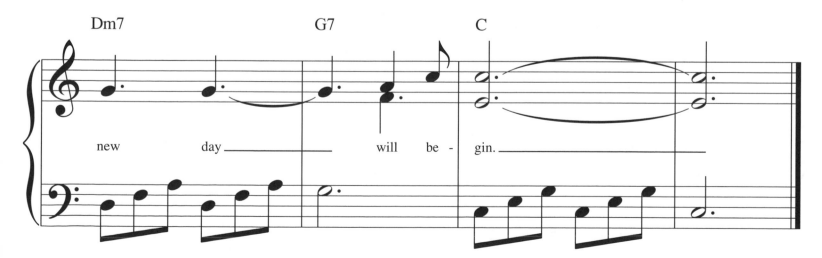

THE MUSIC OF THE NIGHT
from THE PHANTOM OF THE OPERA

Music by ANDREW LLOYD WEBBER
Lyrics by CHARLES HART
Additional Lyrics by RICHARD STILGOE

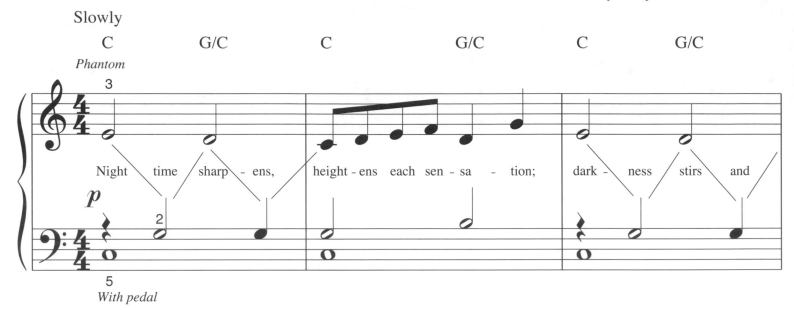

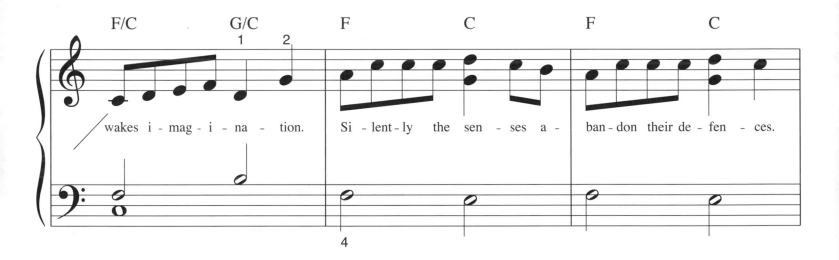

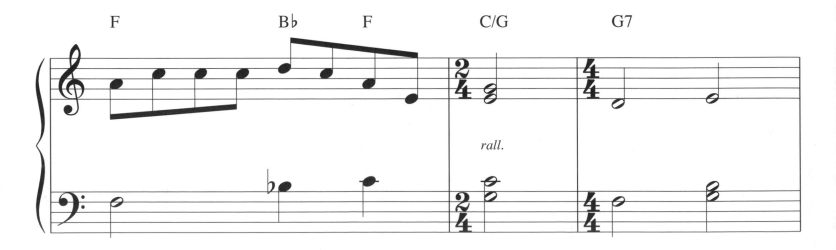

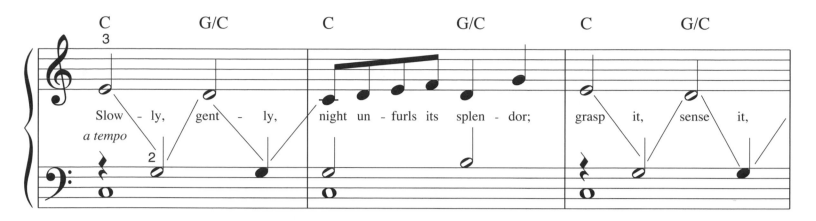

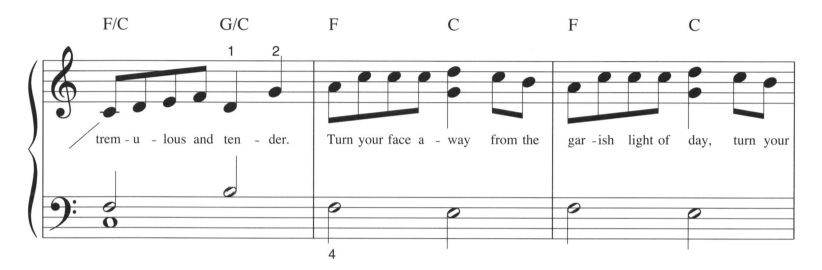

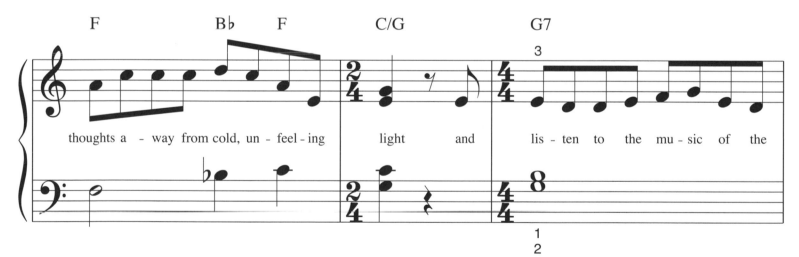

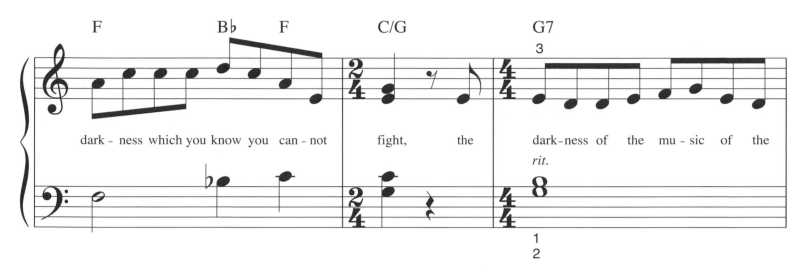

dark - ness which you know you can - not fight, the dark-ness of the mu - sic of the *rit.*

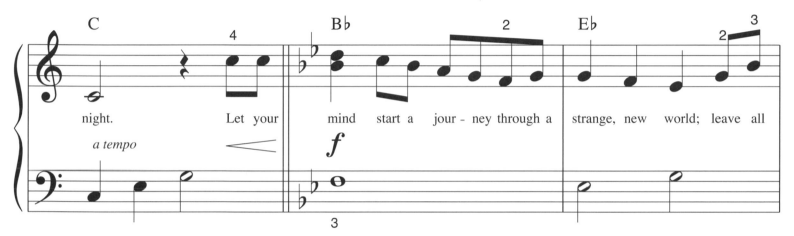

night. Let your mind start a jour - ney through a strange, new world; leave all

a tempo *f*

thoughts of the world you knew be - fore. Let your

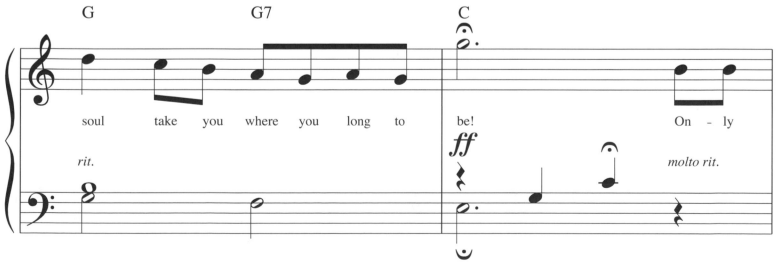

soul take you where you long to be! On - ly

rit. *ff* *molto rit.*

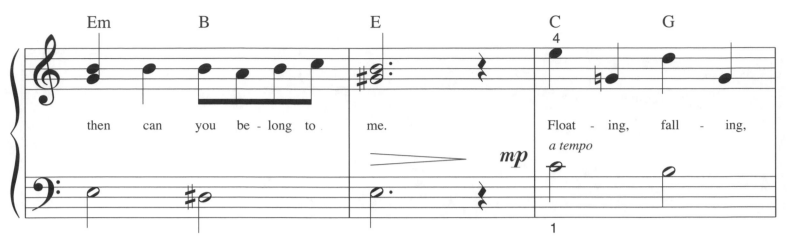

then can you be - long to me. Floating, falling, sweet in - tox - i - ca - tion.

Touch me, trust me, sa - vor each sen - sa - tion.

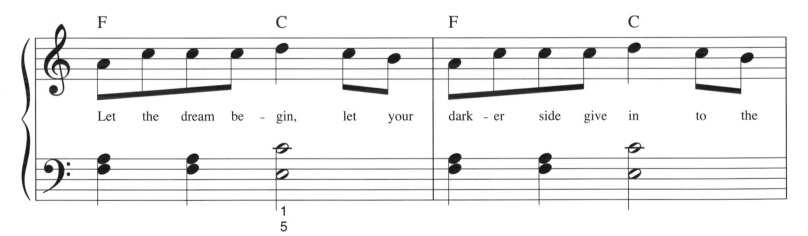

Let the dream be - gin, let your dark - er side give in to the

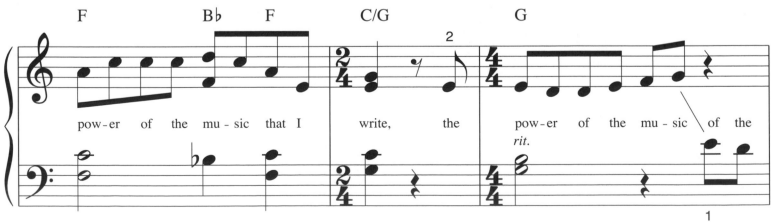

pow - er of the mu - sic that I write, the pow - er of the mu - sic of the

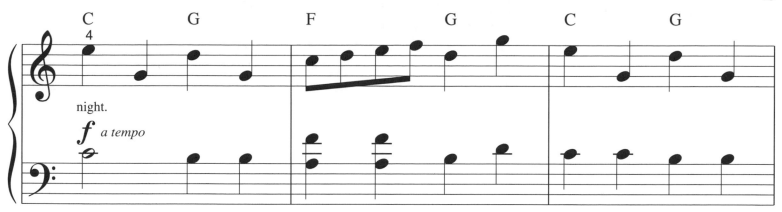

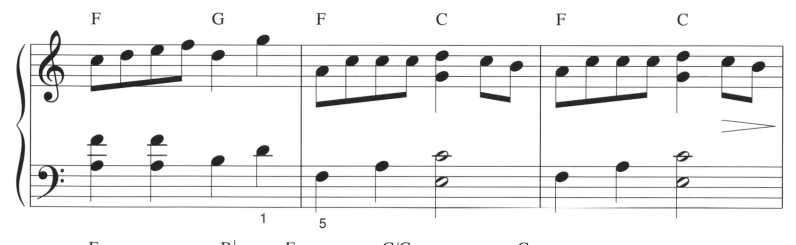

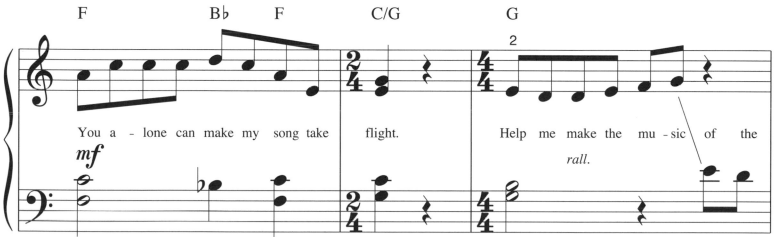

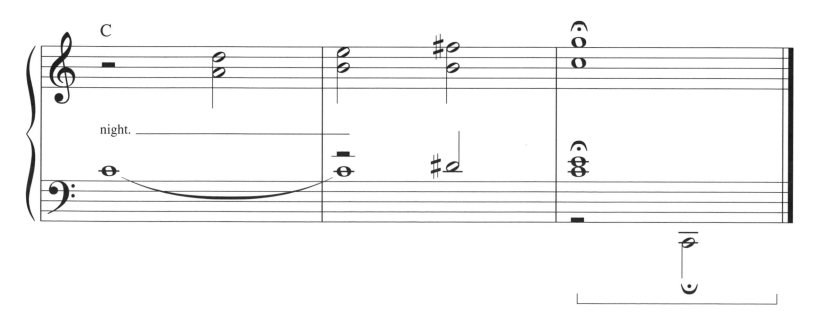

THE PHANTOM OF THE OPERA
from THE PHANTOM OF THE OPERA

Music by ANDREW LLOYD WEBBER
Lyrics by CHARLES HART
Additional Lyrics by RICHARD STILGOE
and MIKE BATT

Moderately fast

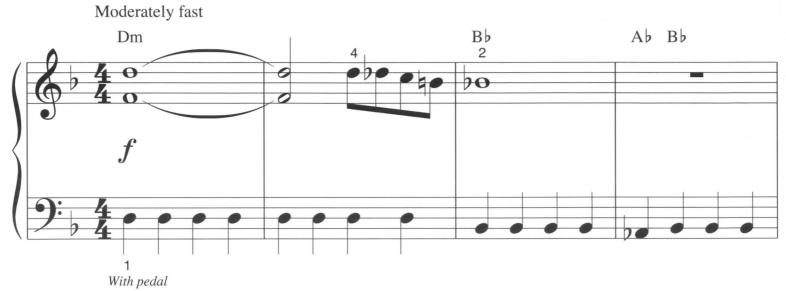

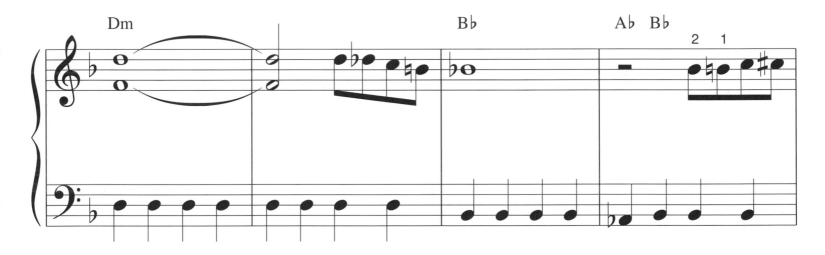

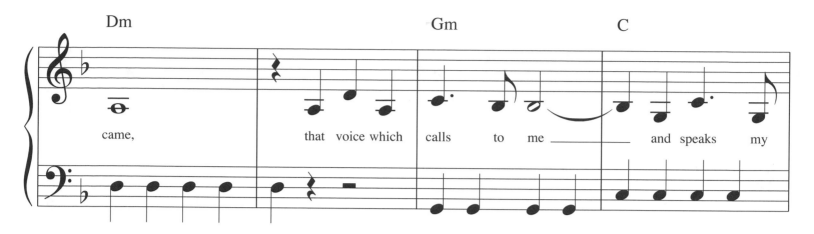

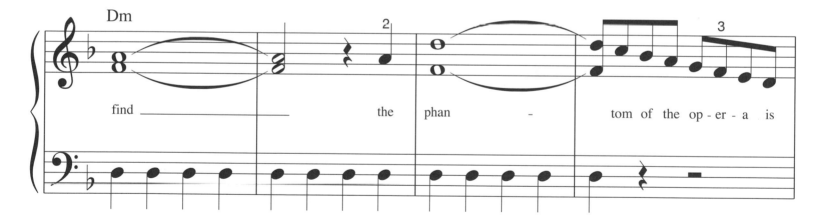

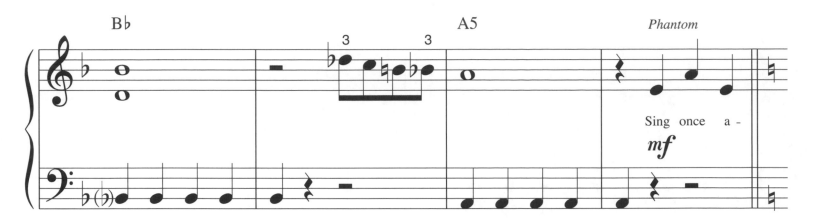

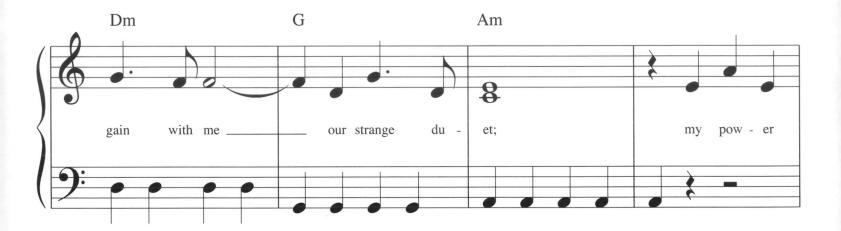

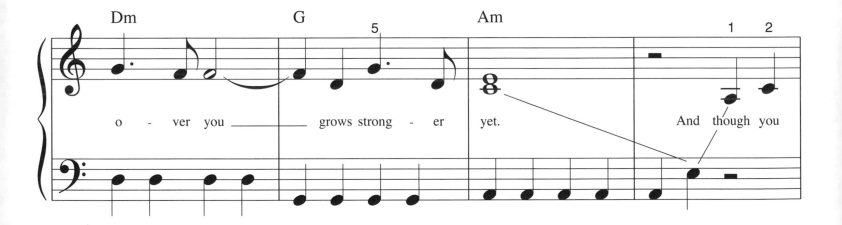

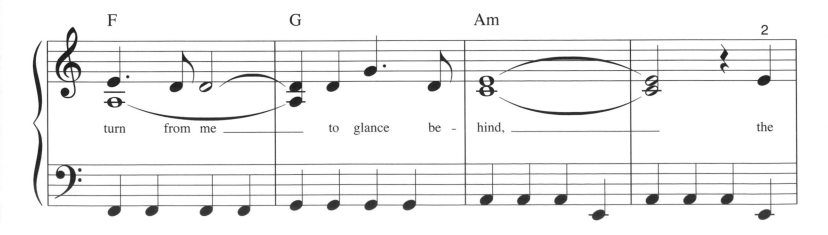

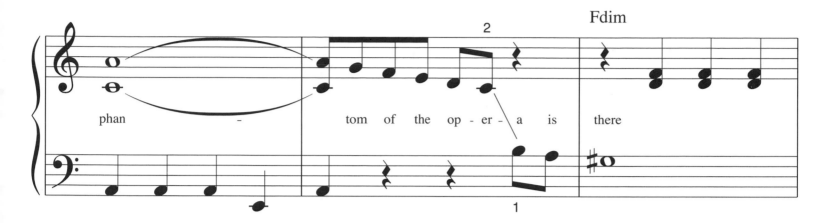

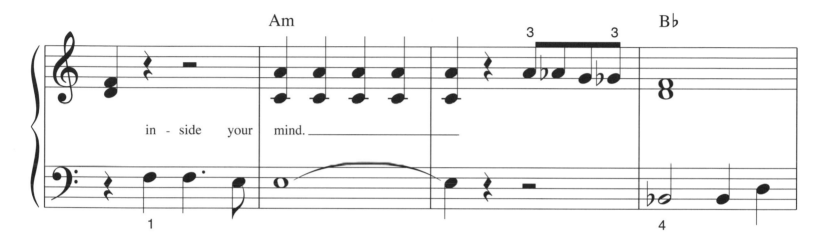

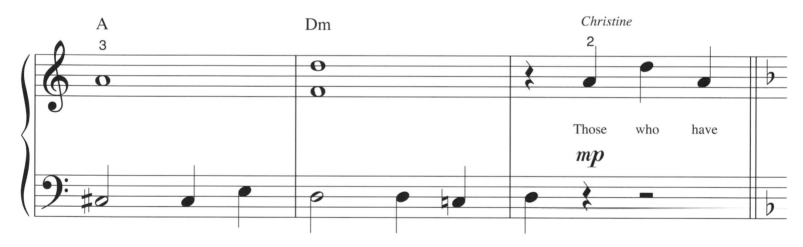

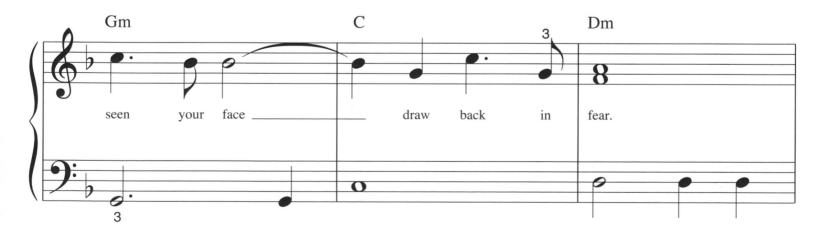

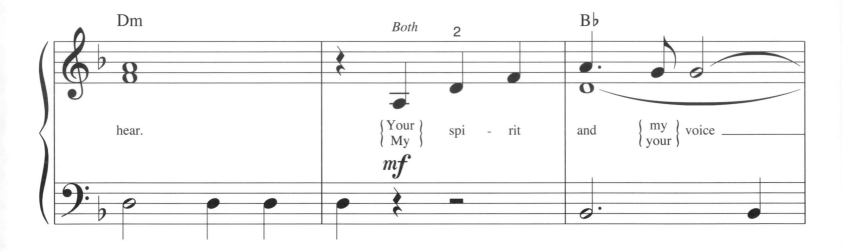

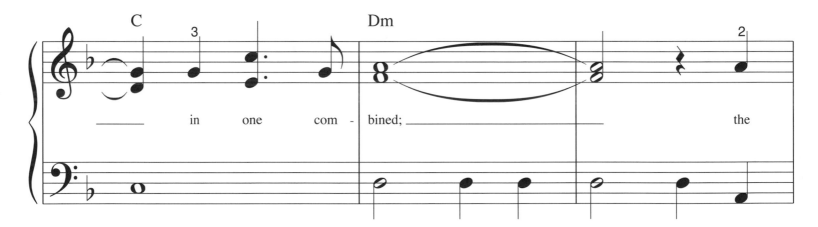

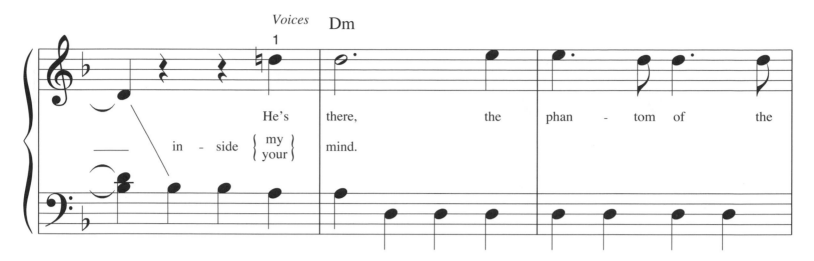

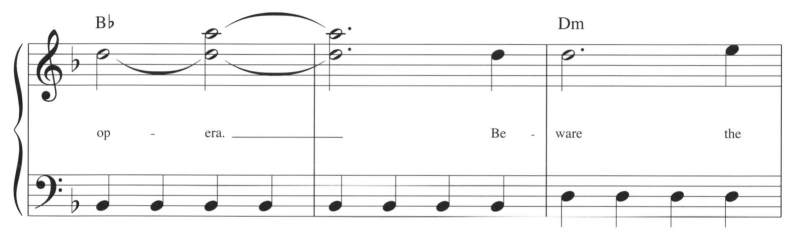

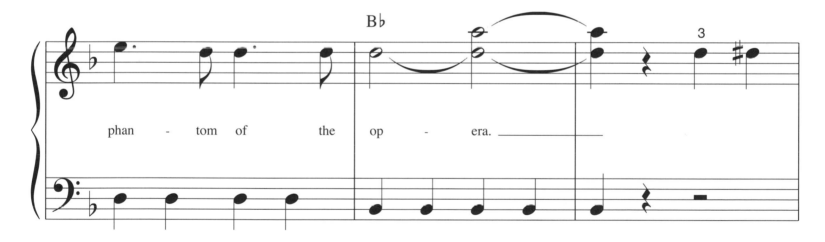

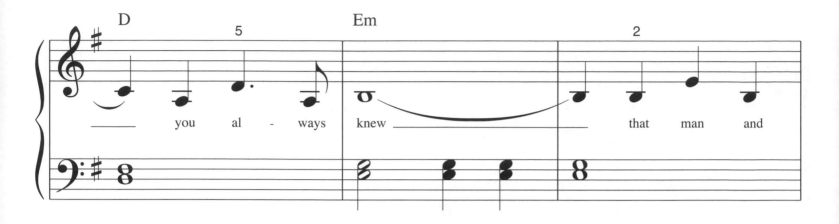

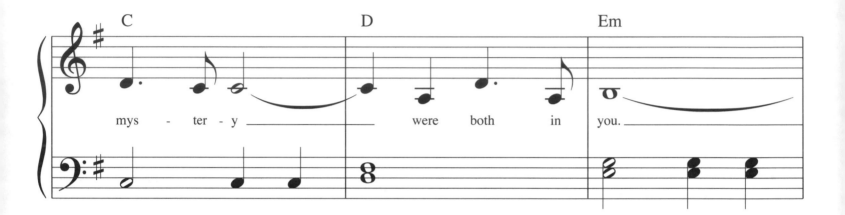

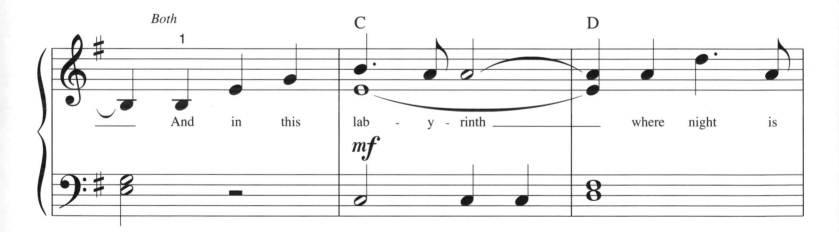

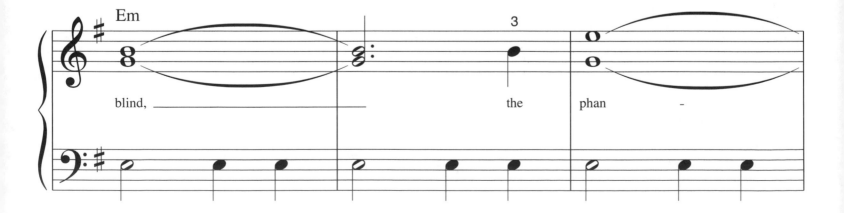

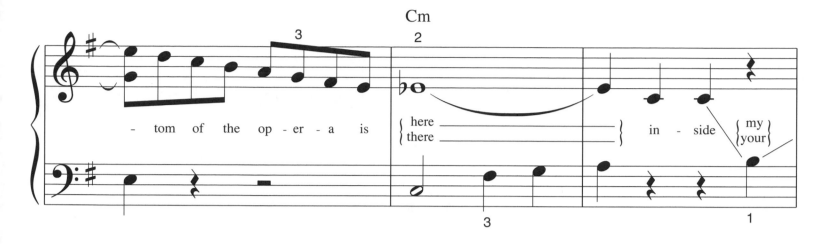

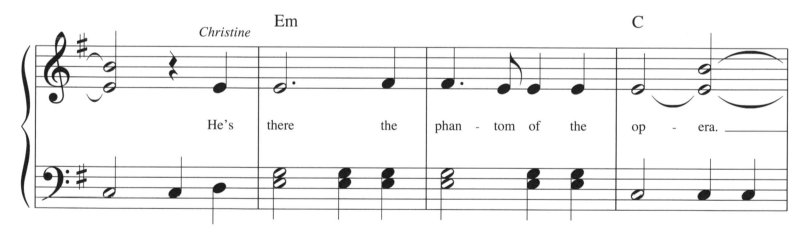

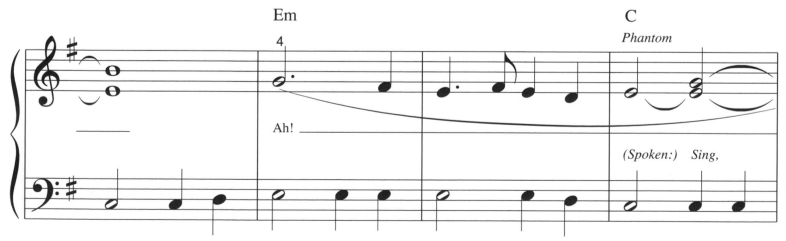

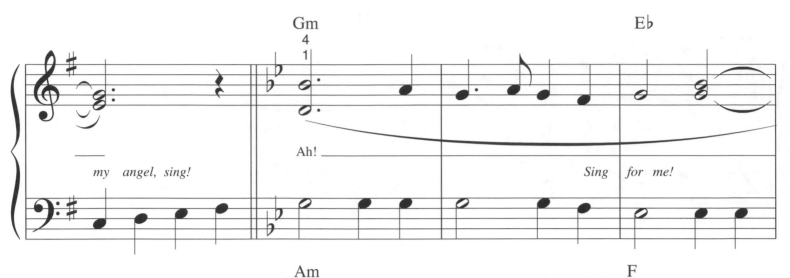

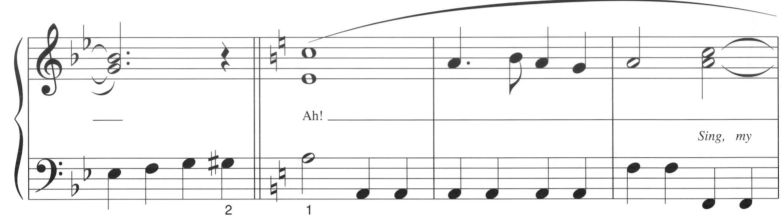

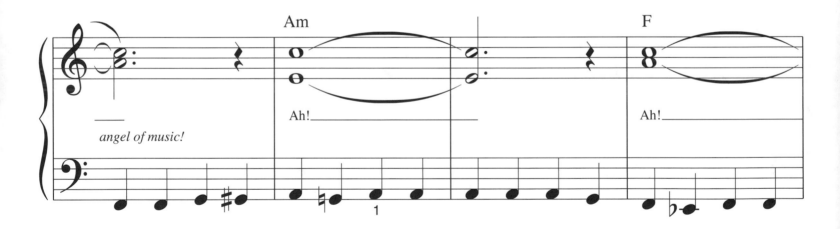

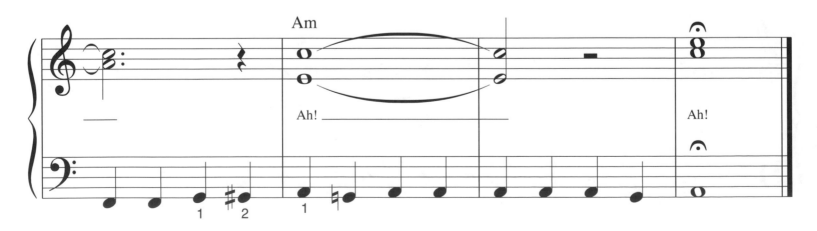

PIE JESU
from REQUIEM

By ANDREW LLOYD WEBBER

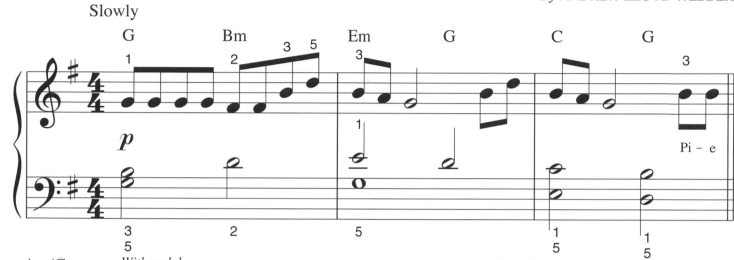

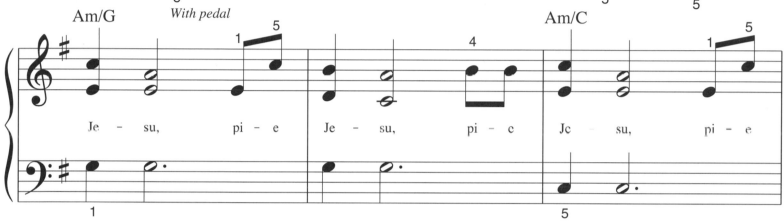

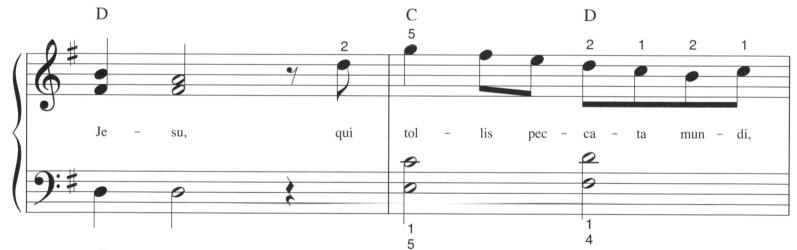

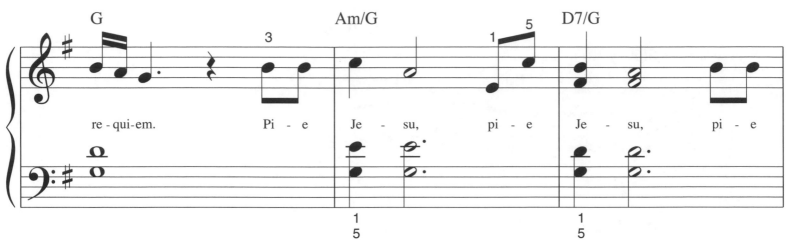

re - qui - em. Pi - e Je - su, pi - e Je - su, pi - e

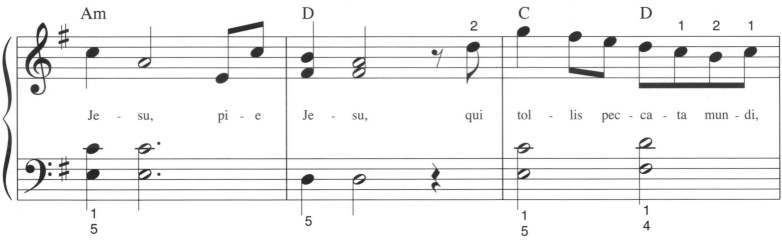

Je - su, pi - e Je - su, qui tol - lis pec - ca - ta mun - di,

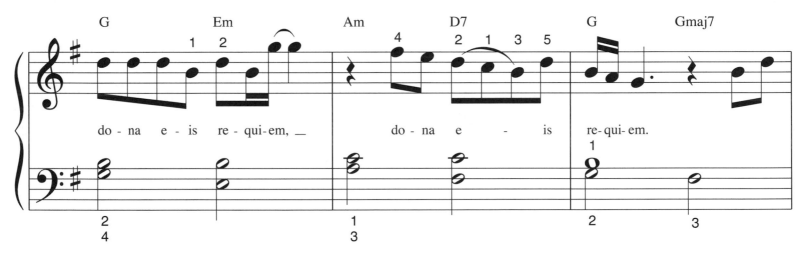

do - na e - is re - qui - em, __ do - na e - is re - qui - em.

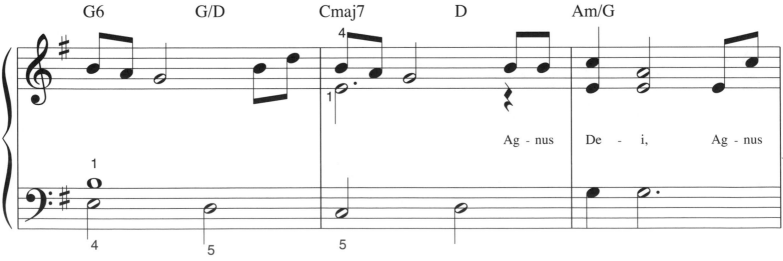

Ag - nus De - i, Ag - nus

SUPERSTAR

from JESUS CHRIST SUPERSTAR

Words by TIM RICE
Music by ANDREW LLOYD WEBBER

Majestically

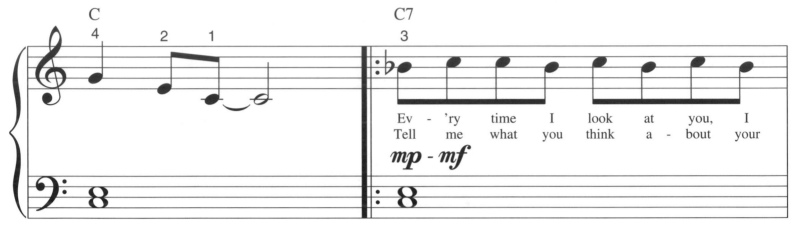

Ev - 'ry time I look at you, I
Tell me what you think a - bout your

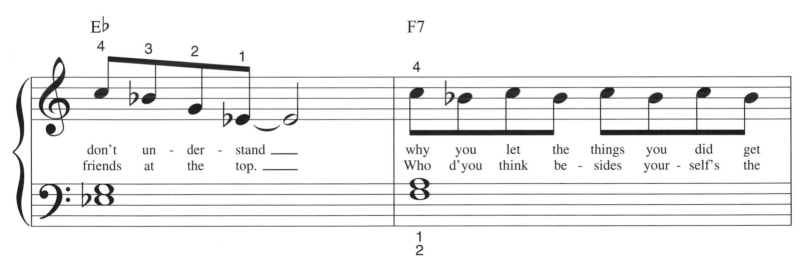

don't un - der - stand ____
friends at the top. ____

why you let the things you did get
Who d'you think be - sides your - self's the

so out of hand. ____
pick of the crop? ____

You'd have man - aged bet - ter if you'd
Bud - dah was he where it's at, is

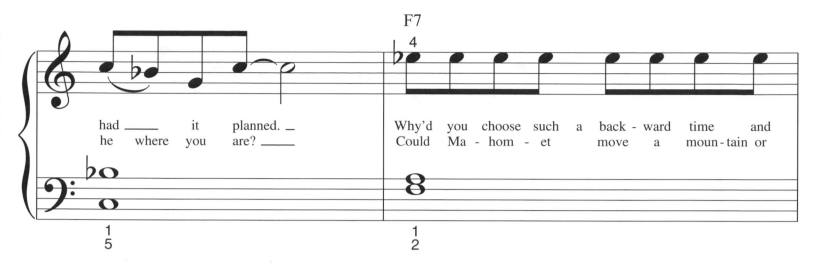

had _____ it planned. _____
he where you are? _____

F7
Why'd you choose such a back-ward time and
Could Ma - hom - et move a moun-tain or

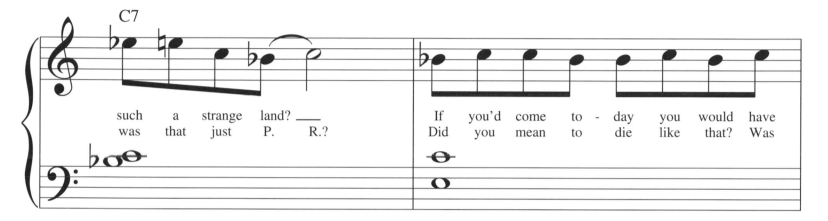

C7
such a strange land? _____
was that just P. R.?

If you'd come to - day you would have
Did you mean to die like that? Was

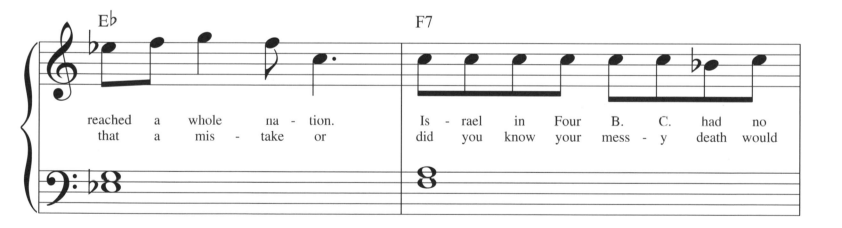

Eb
reached a whole na - tion.
that a mis - take or

F7
Is - rael in Four B. C. had no
did you know your mess - y death would

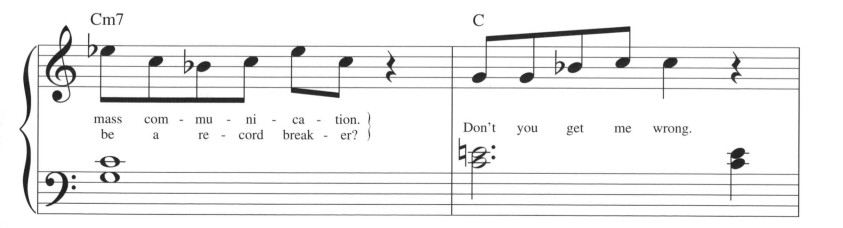

Cm7
mass com - mu - ni - ca - tion.
be a re - cord break - er?

C
Don't you get me wrong.

Don't you get me wrong. Don't you get me wrong.

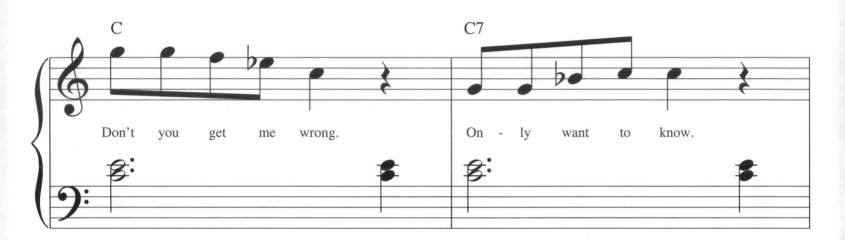

Don't you get me wrong. On - ly want to know.

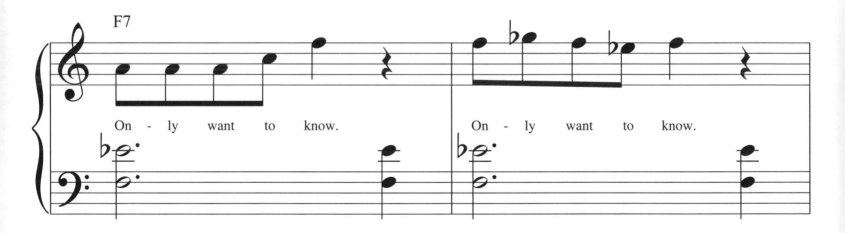

On - ly want to know. On - ly want to know.

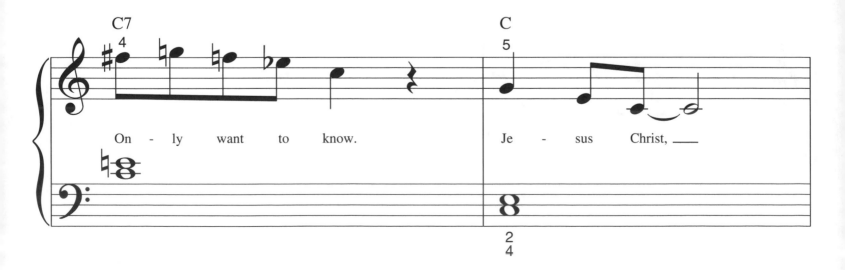

On - ly want to know. Je - sus Christ, ___

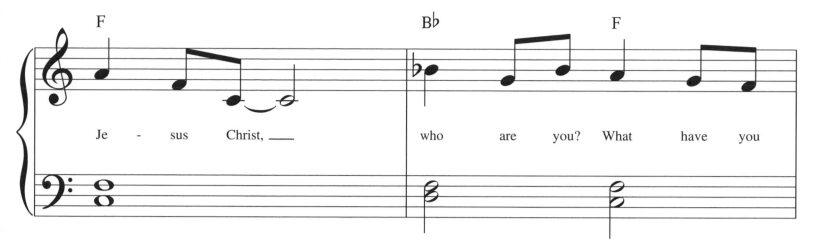

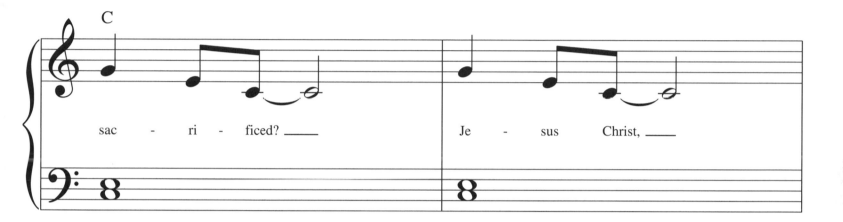

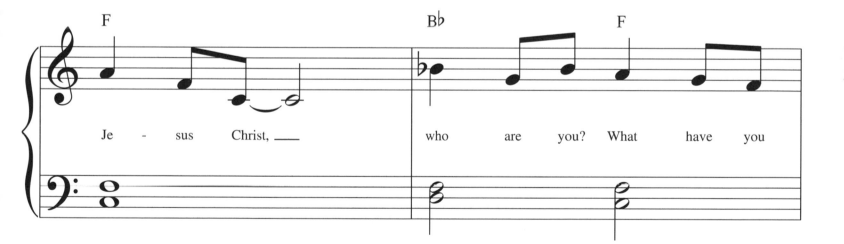

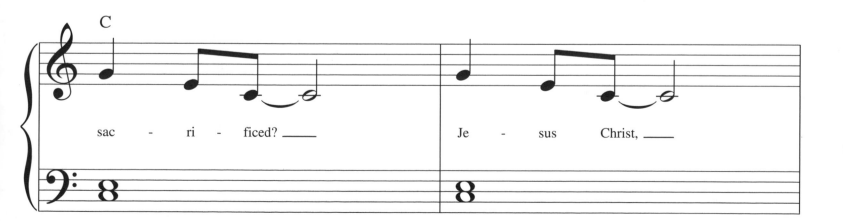

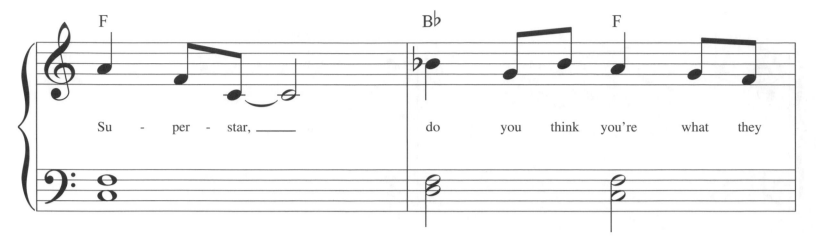

Su - per - star, _____ do you think you're what they

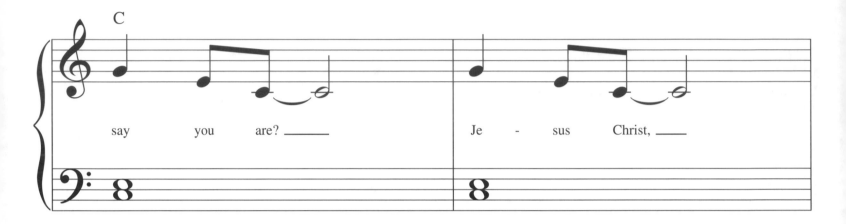

say you are? _____ Je - sus Christ, _____

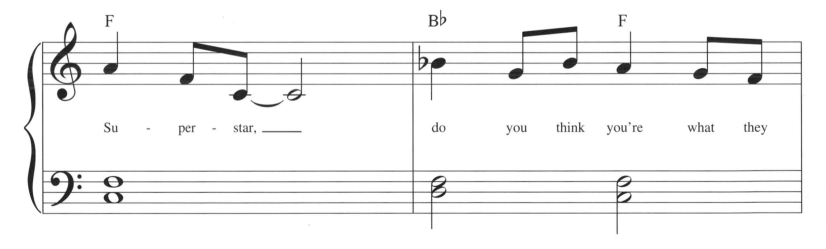

Su - per - star, _____ do you think you're what they

say you are? _____

3 2

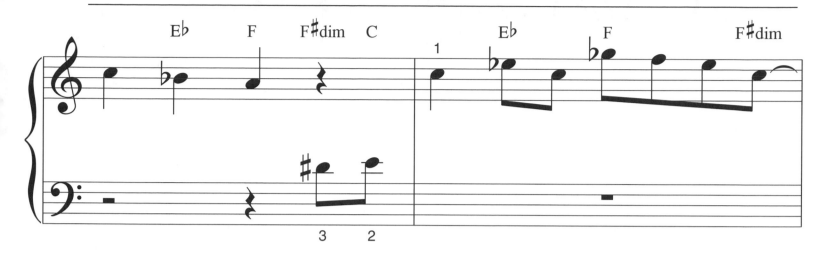

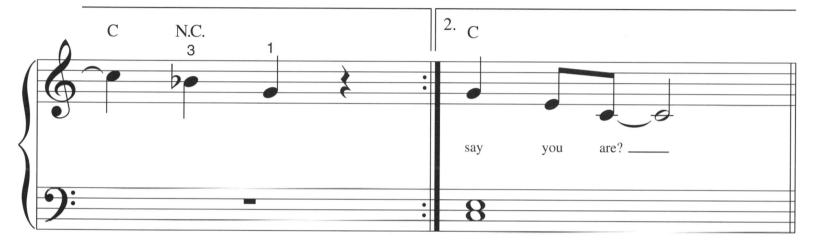

say you are? _____

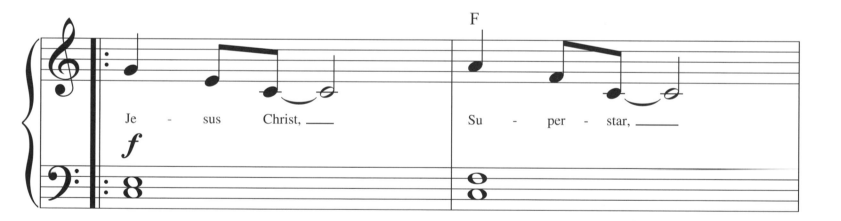

Je - sus Christ, _____ Su - per - star, _____

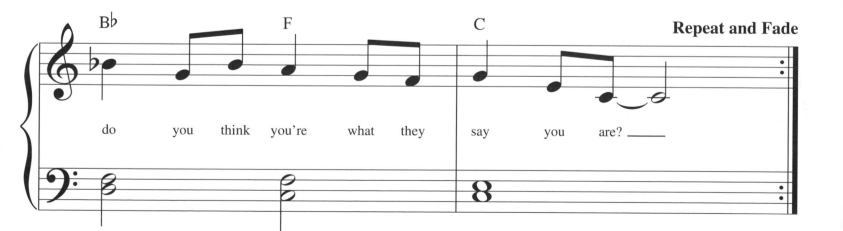

Repeat and Fade

do you think you're what they say you are? _____

TAKE THAT LOOK OFF YOUR FACE

from SONG & DANCE

Music by ANDREW LLOYD WEBBER
Lyrics by DON BLACK

Moderately

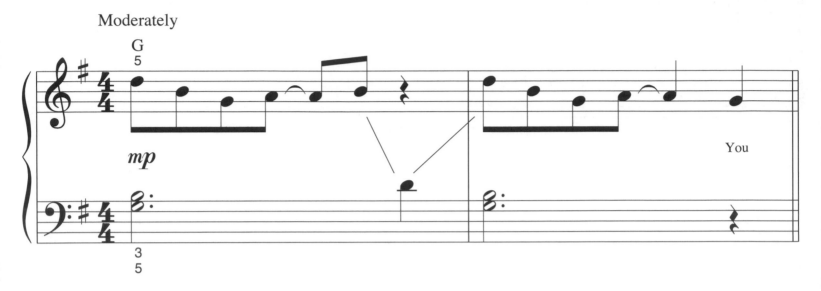

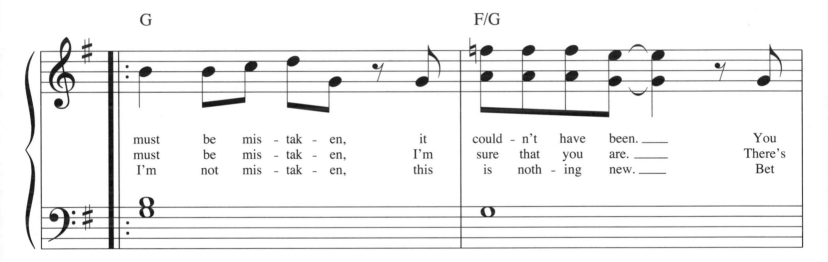

must be mis-tak-en, it
must be mis-tak-en, I'm
I'm not mis-tak-en, this

could-n't have been. ____
sure that you are. ____
is noth-ing new. ____

You
There's
Bet

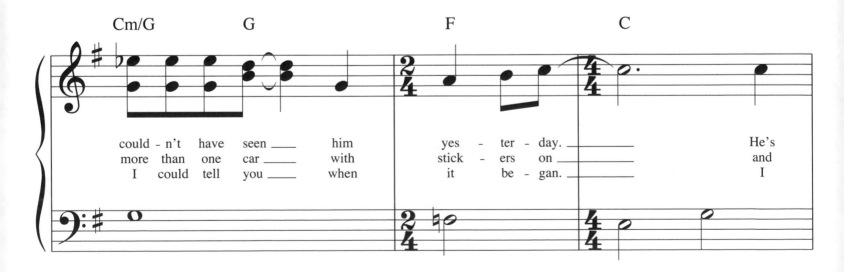

could-n't have seen ____ him
more than one car ____ with
I could tell you ____ when

yes-ter-day. ____
stick-ers on ____
it be-gan. ____

He's
and
I

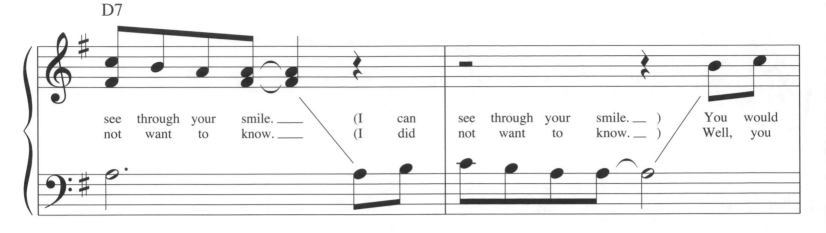

see through your smile. ____ (I can
not want to know. ____ (I did

see through your smile. __) You would
not want to know. __) Well, you

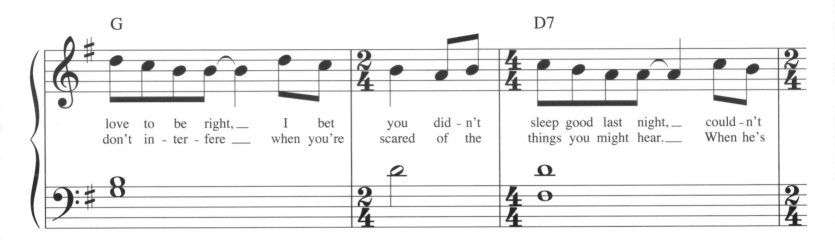

love to be right, __ I bet
don't in - ter - fere __ when you're

you did - n't
scared of the

sleep good last night, __ could - n't
things you might hear.__ When he's

wait to bring
back, you think

all of that bad __ news to my
I will end it ____ right there and

door. Well, I've
then. Well, my

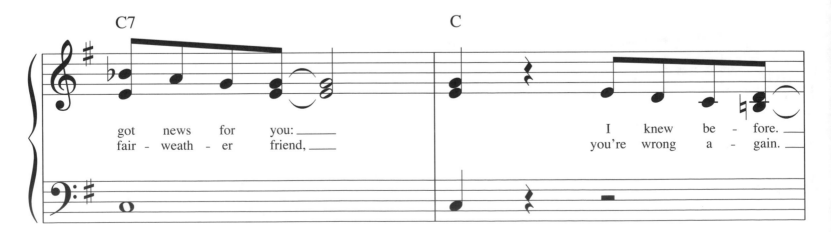

got news for you: _____
fair - weath - er friend, ____

I knew be - fore. ____
you're wrong a - gain. ____

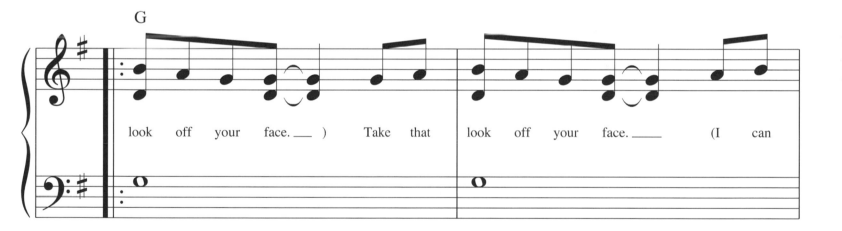

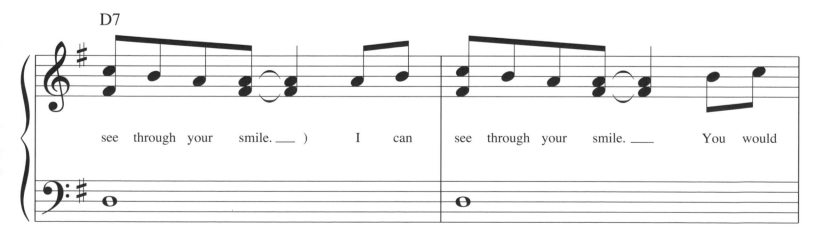

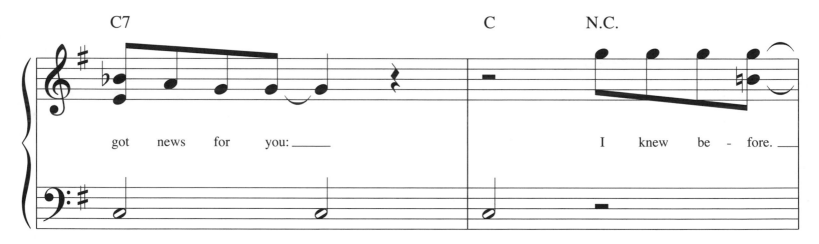

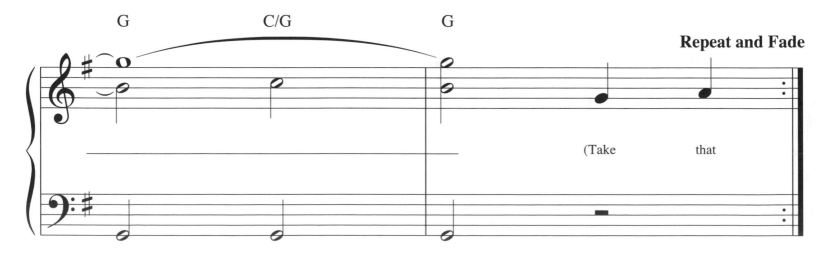